GOLD COUNTRY

HOW TO USE THIS GUIDEBOOK

This guidebook is divided into five sections: *An Introduction to the Gold Country, The Gold Rush, Southern Gold Country, Northern Gold Country* and *Sacramento.*

The first two sections comprise essays, designed to provide you with facts on the area.

In the next three sections we explore the Gold Country, with a detailed, geographical breakdown of the area. Each section contains descriptions of the various places and points of interest, followed by a sub-section entitled *Practical Information*. The *Practical Information* is designed to provide you with a ready reference to accommodations, restaurants, tours, places of interest, recreation areas, transportation, etc., with addresses and phone numbers.

A quick and easy way into this book is the *Index* at the end.

Titles in this Series

The Complete Gold Country Guidebook
The Complete Lake Tahoe Guidebook
The Complete Wine Country Guidebook
The Complete Monterey Peninsula Guidebook
Vacation Towns of California
Farm Tours of Northern California
The Complete San Francisco Guidebook

Indian Chief Travel Guides are available from your local bookstore or Indian Chief Publishing House, P.O. Box 5205, Tahoe City, CA 95730.

The Complete
GOLD COUNTRY
Guidebook

Published by Indian Chief Publishing House
Tahoe City, California

Area Editor: **B. SANGWAN**
Editorial Associate: **PHILLIPPA J. SAVAGE**
Photographs: **Leroy Radanovich**
    (Campo Seco photo by Plez Hill)

ISBN 0-916841-14-6

Printed in the U.S.A.

CONTENTS

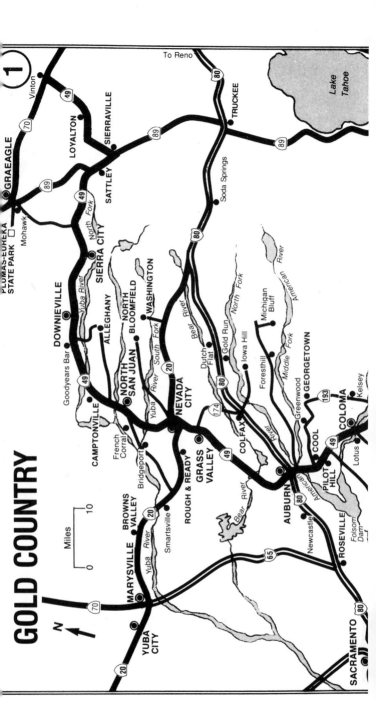

GOLD COUNTRY

N

Miles
0   10

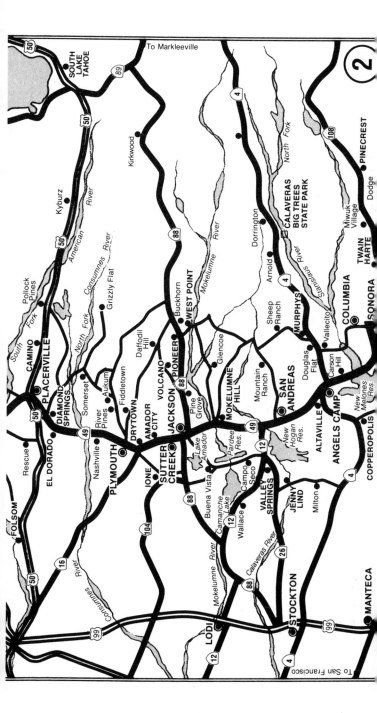

To Markleeville

SOUTH LAKE TAHOE

PINECREST

Kirkwood

Dodge

Kyburz

CALAVERAS BIG TREES STATE PARK

North Fork

Miwuk Village

TWAIN HARTE

American River

Pollock Pines

Dorrington

Consumnes River

Arnold

Grizzly Flat

COLUMBIA

SONORA

CAMINO

Mokelumne River

Stanislaus River

PLACERVILLE

Buckhorn

WEST POINT

Sheep Ranch

DIAMOND SPRINGS

Somerset

Daffodil Hill

MURPHYS

Vallecito

Carson Hill

River Pines

Aukum

Fiddletown

VOLCANO

Glencoe

Douglas Flat

EL DORADO

AMADOR CITY

PIONEER

Pine Grove

MOKELUMNE HILL

Mountain Ranch

SAN ANDREAS

ANGELS CAMP

Rescue

Nashville

DRYTOWN

JACKSON

ALTAVILLE

New Melones Res.

PLYMOUTH

SUTTER CREEK

Lake Amador

Pardee Res.

COPPEROPOLIS

FOLSOM

IONE

Buena Vista

Campo Seco

San Hogan Res.

VALLEY SPRINGS

JENNY LIND

Milton

Camanche Lake

Wallace

Mokelumne River

Calaveras River

Consumnes River

STOCKTON

MANTECA

LODI

To San Francisco

7

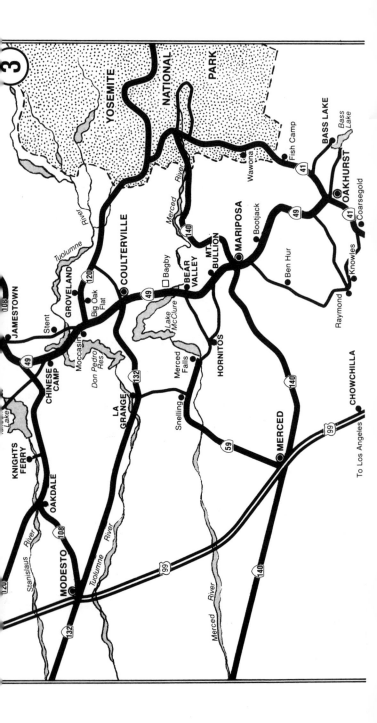

YOSEMITE NATIONAL PARK

BASS LAKE
Bass Lake

Fish Camp

Wawona

OAKHURST

Coarsegold

MARIPOSA

Bootjack

Knowles

MT. BULLION

Ben Hur

BEAR VALLEY

Raymond

COULTERVILLE

Bagby

Merced River

HORNITOS

CHOWCHILLA

GROVELAND

Big Oak Flat

Lake McClure

Merced Falls

To Los Angeles

JAMESTOWN

Stent

Moccasin

Don Pedro Res.

LA GRANGE

Snelling

MERCED

CHINESE CAMP

Tuolumne River

KNIGHTS FERRY

OAKDALE

Stanislaus River

MODESTO

Tuolumne River

Merced River

8

AN INTRODUCTION TO THE GOLD COUNTRY

The Gold Country is rich, historically and scenically. In 1848 it was the scene of the great California Gold Rush. It yielded almost $2.5 billion in gold between 1848 and 1958: gold that built the West — and the city of San Francisco — and gave California its economic base. It also gave California its illustrious title, "The Golden State."

The Gold Country is over 300 miles long and several miles wide, lying along the western slopes of the Sierra Nevada mountain range, some 150 miles east of San Francisco. It is made up of nine different counties: El Dorado, Placer, Nevada, Sierra, Amador, Calaveras, Tuolumne, Mariposa and Madera. It has a similar number of major rivers flowing through it — American, Yuba, Bear, Feather, Consumnes, Mokelumne, Stanislaus, Tuolumne and Merced. It also contains over 100 picturesque old towns and villages — some of the oldest and most colorful in California, with names like Hangtown, Fiddletown, Rough and Ready, Volcano, Drytown and Jackass Hill. Most of these further contain scores of historic relics: adobe structures, frame cottages, fireproof stone and brick buildings, and splendid Victorians. There are, in fact, over 1,000 such relics yet there.

The Gold Country also has great scenic variety, with elevations ranging from around 900 feet to over 7,000 feet. In the south are rolling golden hills, dotted quite consistently with ancient oaks and heavenly locust trees. In the north the countryside is distinguished by its soaring evergreens and majestic granite peaks which often rise above 8,000 feet. The climate, accordingly, is supremely varied — with temperatures ranging from 100° in August in the southern regions, to around 32° in January in the north's mountainous, often snow-covered, terrain.

Travel to, and in, the Gold Country is surprisingly easy. Most of its towns are strung along the well-maintained 316-mile Mother Lode Highway (appropriately numbered "49," for the great year of the Gold Rush). Several other good roads and highways — such as the all-important Interstate 80, and Highways 50, 88, 20, 108, 120, 140, 132, 4 and 41 — intersect Highway 49 at various points, making all the different parts of the gold region easily accessible.

Visitor information, too, is readily available throughout the Gold Country. There are, in addition, over 100 bed and breakfast inns and historic hostelries and an abundance of comfortable motels and fine restaurants in the area. There are also 30 most excellent museums here, and a vast array of recreational facilities, including fishing, boating, swimming, wind-surfing, water-skiing, hiking, camping, horseback riding, gold panning, wine tasting, golf, bicycling and even skiing.

Indeed, the Gold Country is one of the most unique all-season vacation areas in the West, historic and scenic, vast and varied — with warm-water lake resorts and snowy mountain slopes, all within an hour's drive.

THE GOLD RUSH

A Grand Adventure

On January 24, 1848, the first traces of gold were discovered in the American River at a remote valley in the Sierra Nevada foothills, known as Coloma. The discovery set off what became the greatest gold rush in history. Gold seekers journeyed from every corner of the globe to the gold fields of California. Americans from the East Coast traveled overland across the vast desert plains, or voyaged around Cape Horn; English, Welsh, French and other Europeans sailed into the San Francisco bay by the thousands, as did boat-loads of Australian convicts known as the "Sydney Ducks." Mexicans, Chileans and Peruvians crossed over into California from the south, and were the most numerous of the "foreign miners"; and Chinese, brought over on ships from Hong Kong as indentured workers, gradually filtered into the foothills country, too. In a little over two years, 1848-1850, California's non-Indian population ballooned from 2,000 to a staggering 100,000, and by 1852 nearly 300,000 hopeful souls were working the Sierra rivers and streams.

The first to arrive in the gold fields were the pioneer farmers and settlers who had come to California in the early 1840s. They found gold in such abundance in the virgin hills that one ex-farmer, writing to friends in Illinois, boasted: "We in this country live and move on beds of the richest minerals . . . We are in our infancy in wealth. It is but dawning so far as mines and rich ores are concerned. We have them for picking up."

The early months, however, generated little enthusiasm and much skepticism among those yet on the "outside." Then, on May 12, 1848, Sam Brannan, a former Mormon leader and later California's first millionaire, returned from Coloma to San Francisco, waving a bottle full of gold dust and shouting: "Gold! Gold! Gold from the American River!" The sight of the gold and Brannan's exuberance electrified the city. Ordinary people, men with families and property, abandoned their homes and jobs and rushed to the gold fields. In a matter of days boom town San Francisco became deserted, and on May 29 the city's respected newspaper, the *Californian*, in its last issue, lamented: "The whole country from San Francisco to Los Angeles and from the seashore to the Sierra Nevada resounds to the sordid cry of gold, gold!, GOLD! while the field is left half planted, the house half built and everything neglected but the manufacture of shovels and pickaxes."

In December, 1848, the Gold Rush gathered still more momentum, when President Polk, speaking before the United States Congress at Washington, D.C., officially endorsed the news from California. He declared: "I have no hesitation in saying that there is more gold in the country drained by the Sacramento and San Joaquin rivers than will pay the cost of the war with Mexico a hundred times over." (The war with Mexico, in which the United States had wrested the territory of California, had, quite ironically, been fought only the previous year, and the treaty signed just nine days after the gold discovery which, briefly, was kept secret by the original discoverer, James Marshall, and the man on whose holdings the gold had been found, John Sutter.)

In 1849 the rush to riches began in earnest. Overland wagon-trains began rolling westward; ships in New York set sail for the Pacific Coast; and argonauts in Chile, Peru, Hawaii, and ports throughout Europe prepared for voyage to the golden land. Summing up the scene, in January of that year, the New York City *Herald* reported: "All classes of our citizens appear to be under the influence of this extraordinary mania . . . All are rushing towards that wonderful California which sets the public mind almost on the highway to insanity . . . Every day men of property and means are advertising their possessions for sale in order to furnish themselves with means to reach that golden land."

Those who arrived in California in 1849 were known to the world as the "Forty-niners" — the celebrated heroes of the mid-19th century. They nurtured some of the most fascinating legends and lore, and opened up California's gold regions in a time span previously unimaginable. Between 1849 and the early 1850s, no fewer than 500 boisterous towns and camps sprang up throughout the foothills, with such whimsical names as Rattlesnake Bar, Murderers Bar, Shirttail, Slumgullion, Freezeout and Humbug. A town was born wherever a "strike" was made, and dismantled just as the "color" — yellow, dazzling gold — ran out. Frequently miners would abandon moderately profitable claims with the news — often rumors — of a "big strike" elsewhere. In fact, this trait was so common among the Forty-niners that a popular tale circulated in the gold camps: Briefly, it was the story of a prospector who went to Heaven but was stopped at the Pearly Gates by St. Peter and told that there was no more room in Heaven, for it had been filled by other prospectors. The new arrival nevertheless persisted. He convinced St. Peter that he could rid Heaven of some of those other prospectors, whereupon he was admitted, provisionally. He then circulated among the others word of a rich, new "strike" in Hell, and within minutes the rush was on — from Heaven to Hell. But the lone prospector soon became uneasy himself, and said to St. Peter that although he had started the rumor, it was entirely possible that there was indeed gold in Hell. So he, too, departed — for Hell.

After the initial years of excitement, however, it became increasingly difficult to "strike it rich" in California's gold country. Thousands of prospectors were swarming in the foothills, claims were everywhere, and practically all the alluvial gold was gone. A favorite gold-camp song reflected the general feeling in a simple rhyme — *When I got there the mining ground/Was staked and claimed for miles around.*

Indeed, life in the camps became hard in later years. Miners toiled long hours for small rewards, and what little gold they washed went toward the bare necessities of life. A pound of bread, for instance, cost upwards of $2.00; a pound of butter, $6.00; a pound of pork, $5.00; a pound of cheese, $6.00; a bottle of ale, $8.00; a box of sardines, $16.00. Simple mining tools were even more exhorbitant: as much as $20.00 for a shovel. And a blanket fetched around $100.00!

During the early 1850s nearly 95% of California's population was male, and entertainment came in various forms — fist fights, gambling, and dancing with one another, with the "ladies" sporting armbands for easy identification. Then, too, the Mexican miners introduced to the foothills the traditional bullfight. Red-blooded Americans, desirous of greater action, developed from the bullfight the spectacle of the "bear and bull fight," in which a native California grizzly was usually pitted against one or two bulls. It became an extremely popular spectator sport all through the gold regions. In a typical manouver, the bear would grip the bull in a bear-hug and drag it down to the ground, while the bull would charge the bear and attempt to gore him, tossing upwards. This unique phenomenon later gave rise to the Wall Street jargon: a Bear Market goes down, a Bull Market, up.

The 1850s also produced a rash of bandits and stagecoach robbers. The much-romanticized Robin Hood-type Joaquin Murrieta began his life of crime in 1850 and quickly gained notoriety throughout California's gold country, ranging from Hornitos to the Mokelumne River. Others, Tom Bell, Rattlesnake Dick, Three-Fingered Jack, and Dick Fellows, the spectacularly unsuccessful highwayman, are all well remembered as part of the region's history. And then, in later years, there was also "Black Bart," the most famous of them all, who held up 28 stagecoaches with an unloaded gun, and always said "please" when robbing them.

In 1854, Bret Harte arrived in California, the first of the illustrious gold rush writers. He roamed the gold fields — carrying a cane and wearing patent-leather shoes and boiled shirts — and found the mining camps to be "ugly, unwashed, vulgar, and lawless." Yet, he wrote of them with a keenness, in *M'liss*, "The Outcasts of Poker Flat," and "The Luck of Roaring Camp." Mark Twain arrived some years later, and wrote passionately of the foothills and its inhabitants, devoting much of his *Roughing It* to them. In 1865, he wrote the tale of "The Celebrated Jumping Frog of Calaveras County," which brought him world renown.

By the late 1850s the gold rush had begun to fade. In 1859, the discovery of the Comstock Lode, a fabulously rich silver deposit, at Virginia City, Nevada, set off a reverse rush, west-east. This officially signalled the end of the California gold rush and the glorious Forty-niner era.

The great gold rush of the mid-19th century had produced legends, and fortunes. Leland Stanford, a petty merchant from near Sacramento, made his fortune in gold and went on to become a railroad magnate, Governor of California, U.S. Senator, and founder of a university. George Hearst, father of newspaper tycoon William Randolph Hearst, greatly enhanced the family fortune with his Sheep Ranch Gold Mine near Murphys. Levi Strauss founded his blue-jeans empire, selling canvas pants to miners. Domingo Ghirardelli, of San Francisco chocolate fame, began with a small store-confectionary in Hornitos in the southern gold region. John Studebaker also started out during the gold rush, with a wheelwright shop in Placerville, the profits from which he later used to build his Studebaker Automobile Corporation.

For the vast majority of the Forty-niners, however, the gold rush was the adventure of a lifetime, popularly described as "seeing the elephant" — a phrase embodying the extraordinary experience of the rush to riches, with all its hopes and all its disappointments, its hardships and its excitement.

The years following the gold rush were a period of consolidation (of existing claims) and large scale mining operations. The hydraulic "monitor" — an out-size high-pressure nozzle used to pummel mountainsides with gallons of water until they crumbled and washed down into sluices — had been invented by E.E. Matteson in as early as 1853, and through the 1860s and 1870s hydraulic mining flourished in California, unabated. The Malakoff Diggins, the largest hydraulic gold mine in the world, was created between 1866 and 1884. It measured 7,000 feet in length, 3,000 feet in width and 600 feet in depth.

Other large scale mining operations in California included such famous hardrock gold mines as the Empire, North Star, Idaho-Maryland, Kennedy, Argonaut, and Central Eureka. These operated into the 1940s, when they were finally ordered to close, as "non-essential" industries, for the war effort during World War II.

The Empire Mine reopened after the war and continued to operate for several more years. It spawned a network of 367 miles of underground workings, reaching an inclined depth of over 11,000 feet, and produced in its 107 years of operation an estimated $70 million in gold. When it closed in 1956, it was the largest, deepest and richest hardrock gold mine in California. It was also one of the last of the state's great gold mines to close.

And so ended California's glorious gold mining era, one of the most colorful chapters in the history of the Golden State.

SOUTHERN GOLD COUNTRY

"The Mother Lode"

The Southern Gold Country comprises nearly two-thirds of the entire Sierra gold region, measuring 190 miles from north to south, with roughly 160 miles of it lying astride the fabulous gold vein known as the "Mother Lode," which runs, in an unbroken streak, from Georgetown south to Mariposa.

The Southern Gold Country is made up of six clearly defined areas — the Placerville area, the Jackson area, the Angels Camp area, the Sonora area, the Mariposa area and the Oakhurst area — all lying one below the other, and each representing a gold county. There are, besides, some 90 gold camps and towns here, and five exceptional state historic parks, with a striking variation in scenery that ranges from the typical low-lying golden hills to the rugged High Sierra wilderness just to the east.

There are several different routes to reach the Southern Gold Country, with at least one major highway feeding into each of its six areas. Highway 50, for instance, leads directly to Placerville; 88 goes to Jackson; 4 to Angels Camp; 108 to Sonora; 140 to Mariposa; and 41 to Oakhurst. A commercial airport, the Columbia Airport, lies just to the north of Sonora.

THE PLACERVILLE AREA

It must be right to say that this is the most important area in the Southern Gold Country, lying at the top end of the fabulous Mother Lode belt and comprising the El Dorado County section of the Gold Country. It is also very easy to get to — either on the much traveled Interstate 80 or on Highway 50, the most direct route from Sacramento (25 miles east). Notable towns of this area are Placerville, the largest, Coloma (9 miles north of Placerville), and Georgetown.

Coloma

It would be unthinkable to visit the Gold Country without going first to Coloma, the site of the original gold discovery that sparked off the Gold Rush. A replica of Sutter's Mill, in the tail-race of which those fateful traces of gold were found on the morning of January 24, 1848, stands on the banks of the South Fork of the American River, quite artful in its duplication with hand-hewn beams and mortise-and-tenon joints; it can be seen working on weekend afternoons. Near to the mill is the actual gold discovery site, where the old Sutter's Mill once stood, reached by a short walk down to the river. On a small hill just above town stands the Marshall Monument, set on magnificent, gently sloping grounds with flower-beds and picnic areas; the statue, of course, is that of James Marshall, the discoverer, cast in 1889 in a San Francisco foundry, and now seen pointing toward the discovery site below. Also on the grounds, well worth investigating, is the Marshall Cabin, where James Marshall once had a blacksmith shop.

Coloma is a lovely, slumbering village, with a population of less than 200, but visited by several thousand tourists every year. Nearly three-quarters of it now lies in the 280-acre Marshall Gold Discovery State Historic Park, where one can enjoy some neat, manicured lawns, criss-crossed by good-sized walks and populated with age-old locusts and the native Chinese "Trees-of-Heaven." The grounds are filled with mining artifacts, old buildings, photogenic ruins, and nature exhibits of sorts. On Main Street (Highway 49) are several gold rush buildings worth visiting — the old Coloma Greys Building which once housed the Civil War military unit known as the Coloma Greys; the old Gunsmith Shop where a man named Bekeart started out with a stock of some 400 Colt and Allen revolvers which he had brought with him from New York in 1849; an authentic miner's cabin and a Mormon Cabin; an 1850s Chinese store, and the brick walls of the Bell General Store, dating from 1855. Just back from the highway on Back Street is the Old Coloma Jail, built from native stone in 1865.

Two splendid churches — St. John's Catholic Church and the Emmanuel Methodist-Episcopal Church, dating from 1858 and 1856, respectively — can be visited on Church Street, high on a hill at the southwestern end of town. These can also be booked for weddings by contacting the park authorities. Of note, too, is the old Coloma Coun-

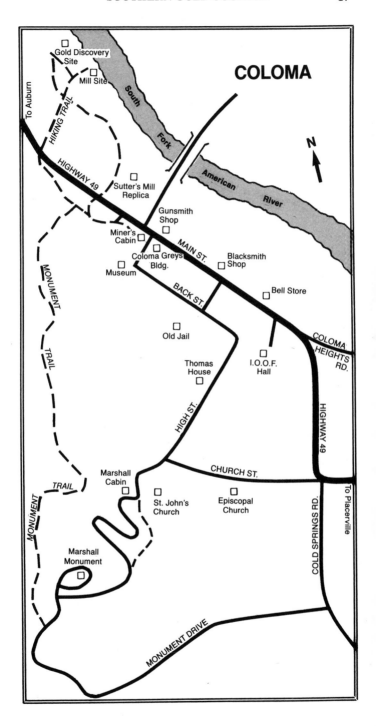

COLOMA

To Auburn

HIKING TRAIL

Gold Discovery Site

Mill Site

South Fork

American River

N

HIGHWAY 49

Sutter's Mill Replica

Gunsmith Shop

Miner's Cabin

MAIN ST.

Coloma Greys Bldg.

Blacksmith Shop

Museum

BACK ST.

Bell Store

MONUMENT

Old Jail

COLOMA HEIGHTS RD.

Thomas House

I.O.O.F. Hall

TRAIL

HIGH ST.

HIGHWAY 49

CHURCH ST.

MONUMENT TRAIL

Marshall Cabin

St. John's Church

Episcopal Church

COLD SPRINGS RD.

To Placerville

Marshall Monument

MONUMENT DRIVE

try Inn, dating from 1857, and the Thomas House, built in 1856 and now restored and furnished as a "typical residence of the 1860s." Both the inn and Thomas House are situated on High Street, just below the hill upon which stand the churches. On Monument Drive, on the way to the Marshall Monument, is the venerable Vineyard House, built in 1878 and now a charming bed and breakfast establishment with a delightful restaurant. In the 1860s, Ulysses S. Grant delivered a campaign speech from the balcony of the Vineyard House.

The park also has a museum, rich in Indian artifacts and mining and nature exhibits, and with an excellent recount of the gold discovery and the stories of John Sutter and James Marshall, the two men so intimately connected with the gold rush, and yet ruined by it — Sutter lost his vast agricultural empire, New Helvetica, to the frenzy of the gold rush, and Marshall, unable to find gold himself, died an embittered and impoverished man at the age of 75. The museum is open 10-5 daily, and the park remains open from 8 a.m. until sunset.

Near to Coloma, just off Highway 49, is the tiny village of Lotus, situated in a beautiful valley and quite popular as a staging point for river-rafting trips and hot-air ballooning. Lotus has a few interesting shops, a schoolhouse that dates from 1869, and the red-brick Adam Lohry Store, dating from 1855 and now housing the Lotus Cafe.

Rescue, farther south from Lotus on the Lotus Road, has a few older buildings dating from the early 1800s when the settlement was a remount station for the Overland Pony Express. Nearby one can visit the 100-year-old Jayhawk Cemetery.

Also of interest, some miles from Coloma on Cold Springs Road (which runs more or less parallel to Highway 49), is Gold Hill, the site of the Wakamatsu Tea and Silk Farm Colony, the first and only Japanese colony in the Mother Lode, established in 1869, and failed within two years of starting. The occasional ruin from the mining days can still be seen here, though the countryside is now given over to fruit growing.

The Georgetown Loop

Highway 193 sets out north toward Georgetown from just outside Placerville, with a scenic ascent over the American River at Chili Bar. But if you are at Coloma, there is a direct access road from there to Garden Valley and on to Georgetown. In any case, both Garden Valley and Kelsey lie to the south of Georgetown, the former an old mining camp of modest proportions, where the Black Oak Mine was an excellent producer of gold during the 1930s. At Kelsey you can see James Marshall's crumbling blacksmith shop, and a plaque that marks the site of the Union Hotel where Marshall died in 1885.

It is roughly six miles from the Garden Valley turnoff on Highway 193 to Georgetown, a robust mountain town abundant in shade trees and old homes. Georgetown was once also known as Growlersburg, because the large gold nuggets found in the streams around here were said to "growl" in the pans. The town's most striking feature, however, is its spacious Main Street, 100 feet wide, so built for fire protection after a series of major fires destroyed the old town, in 1852, 1856, 1858, 1869 and 1897. The Main Street, also, contains several ancient and quite interesting buildings; the out-sized two-story I.O.O.F. Hall, formerly the Balsar House, dating from 1859; the stone-brick Wells Fargo Building & Stagestop, built in 1852; the beautifully restored, wood-frame Georgetown Hotel, dating from 1896 and with an age-old wishing-well beside it; the lovely American River Inn with its wrap-around porch and ornate balconies, which has been operating as a hostelry since 1853; and some other historic buildings, both of wood-frame and stone and brick construction. Near the top end of Main Street on Highway 193 is to be found the Shanon Knox House, dating from 1854 and believed to be the oldest residence in Georgetown. Of interest, too, is the Georgetown Cemetery, located on Highway 193.

West of Georgetown lies Greenwood, which also has a cemetery of some interest, and is surrounded by gentle hillsides that burst forth in a blaze of wild Scotchbroom in springtime. John A. Stone, nicknamed "Old Putt," a song writer and stage performer from the gold rush era, is buried at the Greenwood Cemetery.

Farther still is Cool, a small township situated at the junction of Highways 193 and 49, noted mainly for its limestone quarries and lime kilns. It also has some shops and a restaurant or two. Pilot Hill, the site of the first Grange Hall in California (established 1870), lies just south of Cool on Highway 49, some 4 miles distant. The hill is named for the "pilot" fires that were once burned there to guide pathfinder John Fremont and his party from the valley into the Sierra mountains. The only point of interest at Pilot Hill is a three-story 22-room hotel known as "Baley's Folly," built by Alcander Baley in 1854, at a cost of $20,000, in anticipation of the transcontinental railroad. As it turned out, the railroad was diverted along a different route, and the abandoned hotel now stands as testimony to Baley's judgment.

From Pilot Hill it is another 8 miles or so back to Coloma.

Placerville

8 miles south of Coloma, at the intersection of Highways 49 and 50, lies Placerville, a thriving county seat with associations to several notables from the American past. John Studebaker began his career here as a wheelwright, and with $8,000 in savings he returned to Indiana at the end of the gold rush to found his famous Studebaker Automobile Corporation. Phillip Armour also began here with a small butcher shop, and with an identical sum in savings, $8,000, he too returned to the midwest to establish what became the largest meat-packing empire in the country. Mark Hopkins and Collis Huntington, two of the Big Four who helped finance the Central Pacific Transcontinental Railroad in the 1860s, began their business careers in Placerville with a wagon-load of supplies for miners. "Snowshoe" Thompson also began his illustrious career here, carrying mail bags from Placerville to Genoa, Nevada at the peak of winter on wooden cross-country skis. And poet Edwin Markham ("Man with a Hoe") is buried at the City Cemetery on Chamberlain Street.

Gold was first discovered in Placerville (which was once also known as Hangtown for its rash of grisly lynchings) in 1848, though the town grew mainly as a supply center in the years following the

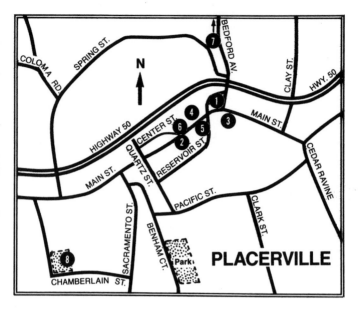

Places of Interest -
1) City Hall & County
   Courthouse
2) Cary House (1860)
3) Museum
4) Old Town Center (1893)
5) Pearson Soda Works
   (1854)
6) Site of Old Hangtree
7) Gold Bug Mine
8) City Cemetery

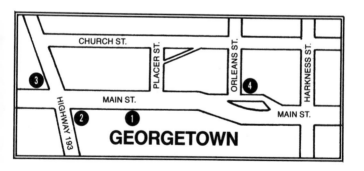

Points of Interest -
1) Georgetown Hotel (1896)
2) I.O.O.F. Hall (1859)
3) Shannon Knox House
   (1851)
4) American River Inn (1853)

discovery of the Comstock Lode in Nevada in 1859. Many of the town's older streets still follow the original mule paths worn down by traders' pack trains more than a century ago, as they converged on the center of town. Main Street is an especially fine example, quite narrow and crooked, with an unusual fork in the center of it, in the midst of which can be seen the town's large, ancient fire bell.

Placerville has a wealth of gold rush era buildings well worth exploring, most of them now housing newer businesses or operating as quaint bed and breakfast establishments. On Main Street one can visit the red-brick Old Town Centre, originally built as a Masonic Lodge in 1893; the City Hall & County Courthouse with its row of splendid arched windows, built in the early 1900s and still in use as a courthouse; the old I.O.O.F. Hall, built from locally quarried stone in 1859; and the Old Fountain & Tallman Soda Works Building, featuring stone and brick construction and dating from 1852. This last, believed to be one of the few buildings to have survived the 1856 fire that leveled much of the original town, now houses the Placerville Historical Museum, where displays are of 19th-century relics and include a most interesting antique washing machine.

Of interest, too, is the three-story red-brick Cary house, with its overhanging balconies, dating from 1860 and located at the corner of Main and Center Streets. It was from the first floor balcony of this hotel that Horace Greeley (made famous in Mark Twain's *Roughing It*) delivered a speech. Briefly, the story of Horace Greeley involves a notorious stagecoach driver, Hank Monk, who treated Greeley to a bone-shattering ride from Carson City, Nevada to Placerville, admonishing, "Keep your seat, Horace, I'll get you there on time!" Near to the Cary House, on the opposite side of the street, is the Hangtown Saloon, built on the site of the town's infamous Hangtree; as a reminder, there is a grisly effigy above the saloon entrance.

In the Bedford City Park at the northern end of town you can tour a real hardrock gold mine, the Gold Bug Mine, where two lighted shafts — 362 feet and 147 feet long, respectively — are open to the public. Remains of a stamp mill can be viewed on a small hill above the mine. The park also has some good picnicking and hiking possibilities.

If you have the time — and the appetite — visit one of the local restaurants and sample the famous Hangtown Fry, a concoction of bacon, eggs and oysters — all fried up together! According to local lore, it was a hungry miner, fresh from a rich strike, who stalked into a diner and demanded to know what the most expensive food items were; when informed that bacon, eggs and oysters were indeed the most expensive, he simply turned to the kitchen help and said, "Fry 'em up." And thus was born the Hangtown Fry.

Before leaving Placerville south on Highway 49, take the time also to visit Apple Hill, a short distance east on Highway 50, where there are some 85 apple orchards, pink and white with apple blossoms in fall. Most of these are open to the public for local sales and picking. Also, near to the orchards are one or two quite interesting wineries, noted for their rich, intense Zinfandels; the Madrona Vineyards are at the foot of Apple Hill at an elevation of 3,000 feet, and the Boeger Winery, established in 1872 and with an ancient stone cellar open to public tours, lies just on the outskirts of Placerville.

Small Towns and A Farm Area

South of Placerville on Highway 49 are the little townships of Diamond Springs and El Dorado, both primarily stagestops on the Carson Emigrant Trail, and each with two or three historically interesting buildings. Diamond Springs has a wood-frame I.O.O.F. Hall dating from 1852.

A short detour west on Highway 50 will take you to Shingle Springs, which also has some restored old buildings, a plaque or two of historical interest, and a mining history that dates from 1850.

South, again, on Highway 49, seven or eight miles from El Dorado, one arrives at Nashville, one of the oldest quartz mining camps in the area, and the site of the first stamp mill in the Mother Lode; the mill was shipped around the Horn from the East Coast and used at the Tennessee Mine. Nashville now only has a tumbledown snack bar and a trailer park, surrounded by acres upon acres of pasture land.

An alternative route, from Diamond Springs south, is through Somerset and Mt. Aukum to River Pines, 10 miles beyond which the small, twisty back-country road rejoins Highway 49 at Plymouth. Somerset, Mt. Aukum and River Pines are all quite delightful — small and rural, centers of El Dorado County's wine-grape growing region, with a dozen or so vineyards and small farms to be seen dotting the surrounding hills. Worthwhile, too, is the 11-mile drive from Somerset to Grizzly Flat, a one-time gold mining camp and now a tiny vacation-home community with one or two Christmas Tree farms that are open to the public.

THE JACKSON AREA

The Amador County — which makes up this area — claims for itself the distinction of being the richest county in the Mother Lode, which alone produced in excess of $160 million in gold. Jackson is the county seat here. Other principal towns in the area include Amador City and Sutter Creek — both of which are noted for their antique shops — and Ione, Plymouth, Drytown, Pioneer, and picturesque Volcano and Fiddletown.

Plymouth and Fiddletown

Northernmost in the area, located on Highway 49, is Plymouth, where the Plymouth Consolidated Mines operated from 1883 to 1947, producing in excess of $13.5 million in gold. Some tailing piles from the mine can still be seen on the east side of the highway as you drive through town.

Plymouth has a small Main Street, west off the highway, with some fine, historically interesting buildings; the Roos Building (1873); the

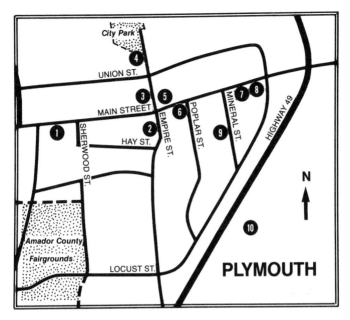

Points of Interest -
1) Old Chinese Store (c.1880)
2) I.O.O.F. Hall (1877)
3) Masonic Temple
4) St. Mary's Catholic Church (1939)
5) Caucasian Hall (1870s)
6) Plymouth Hotel (1929)
7) Old Empire Store
8) Roos Building
9) Native Sons Hall
10) Site of Plymouth Consolidated Mines

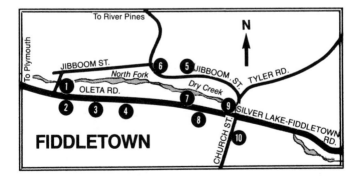

Points of Interest -
1) Chinese Adobe Store (1850s)
2) Chinese Gambling House (1850s)
3) Old Blacksmith Shop
4) Atkinson Store
5) Head House (c.1865)
6) Farnham House (1850s)
7) Community Hall
8) General Store (1850s)
9) Schallhorne Building (1870)
10) Old Schoolhouse (1863)

stone and brick Empire Store, once run by the Empire Mine, forerunner of the Plymouth Consolidated Mines; the Old China Store, a typical Gold Country structure featuring native stone construction, built about 1880; the notable Masonic Temple which originally was a Methodist Church; and the wood-frame Caucasian Hall with its overhanging balcony, built in the 1870s as a meeting place for groups, and now a private residence. On Empire and Mineral streets are the Oddfellows Hall (1877) and the Native Sons Hall, respectively. Also, just south of Plymouth on Highway 49 there is an abandoned brick and stone building, partially in ruin, perhaps the last reminder of Pokerville which grew up side by side with Plymouth in the 1860s. The building was once a Chinese store.

Plymouth is also noted for its splendid fairgrounds where the annual Amador County Fair and Agricultural Show, with its lavish display of vintage farm and ranch equipment, is held each August. Other notable seasonal events held at the fairgrounds include the Shenandoah Valley Grape Festival, which features local wines and cooking of well-known chefs, and the regional Fiddlers' Contest. Plymouth also has some modern shops, a market, and an excellent trailer village.

A worthwhile side trip, 6 miles east from Plymouth on the Fiddletown Road which goes off Highway 49, is the small but lovely Fiddletown, locale of Bret Harte's "An Episode in Fiddletown." It was founded in 1849 by a group of Missourians, and named for the younger members of the group who were said to be "always fiddlin'." For some years afterward, 1878-1932, the town was named Oleta, on the initiative of a local judge embarrassed to write "Fiddletown" as his place of residence. But local groups, proud of their little town, now host the Fiddlers' Jamboree each May at the neighboring Plymouth fairgrounds.

Fiddletown is a mellow sort of village, quite enchanting with its tiny locust-shaded streets and delightful 1850s homes, many with rose bushes and old-fashioned gardens. On Oleta Road, the town's main street, there is an especially charming rammed-earth adobe dwelling dating from 1850, which was once the home of a Chinese herb doctor and where relics of the doctor's trade can still be seen, most of them untouched for over a century. This adobe gem is one of only two of its kind in the state, and is believed to have served as the model for the reconstructed Chinese store at Coloma. Directly across from the store is a Chinese Gambling House (circa 1852), and farther on are the Atkinson Store (1858), a blacksmith shop, and a red-brick general store which has been in continuous operation since it was first built in the 1850s. Of interest, too, is the Schallhorne Building, tallest and largest in town, built in 1870 from locally quarried rhyolite tuff (a light brown stone commonly found in the foothills). There is a well-kept park on the main street as well, with picnicking facilities, a children's playground, and tennis and basketball courts.

Shenandoah Valley

North of Fiddletown lies the fertile Shenandoah Valley, with its small, rounded golden hills and its patchwork of vineyards, interspersed with newly planted walnut orchards. Shenandoah is more or less the heartland of the foothills wine country, which is both the oldest and the newest wine grape growing region in the state. Pioneer European vintners first planted vineyards here in the 1850s and 1860s, but the region was only recently rediscovered, in the 1960s, when the University of California proved the entire region to be ideally suited to the production of premium varietal wine grapes. The area is noted primarily for its rich, intense Zinfandels, although a variety of other wines are produced here as well.

The Shenandoah Valley, besides having one of the oldest vineyards in the region, has the fourth oldest winery in California, the D'Agostini Winery, established in 1856 with 20,000 original vines, some of which are still producing. The winery's old cellar, built from locally quarried stone and hand-hewn beams, and containing handmade oak casks and a display of some rare, antiquated vintners' tools, can be toured during winery hours. Some weathered grape presses, dating from the late 1800s, lie about amid flower-beds, and the winery also has a wine tasting room and picnic area.

There are a dozen or so other wineries in the valley, most of them housed in restored barns and age-old stone cellars, all lying on tiny side roads that branch off the Shenandoah Road. These are mostly small establishments, family owned and operated, and a majority of them are open to visitors for tours and tasting.

Drytown and Amador City

Drytown lies at the intersection of Highways 49, 124 and 16, only three miles south of Plymouth, with one or two smaller back-country roads feeding into it as well. This is the oldest town of record in the county, founded by gold seekers in 1848, but known to John Sutter's farmhands in as early as 1845. The town is named for the creek astride which it is built, and, regardless of what its name may suggest, it was never really a *dry* town, as such; in its heyday, it boasted 26 saloons.

Drytown has a Catholic Church and cemetery, both dating from the 1850s, and an old schoolhouse, believed to be the oldest in the county. Some other buildings of interest include the Butcher Shop-Post Office on the highway, dating from 1851, which has a real marble floor; the Claypiper Theatre, originally built in the 1850s, where the Drytown Claypipers have been performing continuously since 1959; and the Old Brick Store, also dating from the 1850s, where George Hearst, father of newspaper tycoon William Randolph Hearst, had a small press and his mine office. The last of these was also used as an office in later years by cartoonist George McMannus, creator of *Maggie & Jiggs.*

If you have the time, drive along the back road between Drytown and Amador City, where the headframes of two mines, the Fremont and Bunker Hill, can be seen on the hillsides, and ruins of a third, the Little Amador Mine. Bunker Hill produced an estimated $5 million in gold before closing in 1922.

Immediately below Drytown is Amador City, the smallest incorporated city in California, with a population of 202. It is not clear

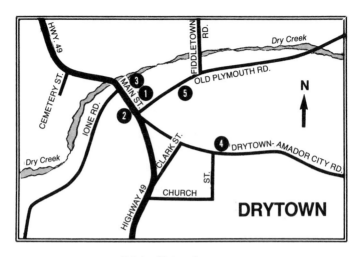

Points of Interest -
1) Claypipers' Theatre
2) Old Brick Store (1850s)
3) Old Butcher Shop
4) Schoolhouse
5) Catholic Church &
   Cemetery

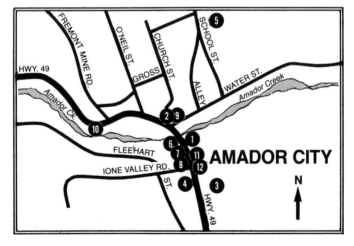

Points of Interest -
1) Amador Hotel (c.1850)
2) Imperial Hotel (1879)
3) Keystone Mine
4) Mine House (1881)
5) Little Amador Mine
6) Kohler Bakery
7) Peyton Bldg. (1879)
8) Weil Bldgs. (1860s)
9) Chichizola Bldg. (1850s)
10) Torres Hall (1899)
11) Kling Bldg. (1878)
12) Fleehart Bldg.

whether Amador City was named for the county or vice versa. In any event, the town dates from 1851, founded by one Jose Maria Amador, a ranchero from the San Ramon valley. The first claim made here was by a Baptist minister, appropriately named "Minister's Claim." The Keystone Consolidated Mine, the headframe of which can be seen at the southern end of town, overhanging a high hill on the east side of the highway, began operating here in 1888, and during its fifty-nine years of operation (it closed in 1947) it produced over $24.5 million in gold. The red-brick office building of the Keystone, the Mine House, dating from 1881, is now a charming bed and breakfast inn, located across from the mine site on the west side of the highway; the inn's guest rooms are named and decorated according to their original function — Vault, Retort, Assay, Directors, and the like.

Amador City has a superb collection of antique shops, housed in beautifully restored gold rush buildings. The Imperial Hotel at the top end of town is especially notable, containing a handful of specialty shops; it dates from 1861 and is unique in that its outer walls are 12 bricks thick at the base, tapering off to a 4-brick thickness at the very top. The wood-frame Amador Hotel, perhaps the oldest in town, is another elegantly restored building, with some assorted and interesting shops within. There is also a winetasting house here, where California wines are featured.

Sutter Creek

A short distance from Amador City is Sutter Creek, the finest town of them all. It is named for the creek upon which it sits, which, in turn, is named for pioneer land baron John Sutter, who camped beside it with a group of Indians in 1848, searching for gold.

We are rather fond of Sutter Creek. It has the smartness and elegance of a New England town, and one of the richest collections of 19th century architecture in the Mother Lode; wood-frame Victorians with overhanging balconies, typical Gold Country buildings with iron shutters and brick fronts, covered and stepped walkways, some boardwalks, one or two turn-of-the-century cast cement buildings, and several neatly-fenced East Coast-style homes, set on lush, tree-shaded grounds. There is even a fine example of Greek Revival architecture: the lovely, steepled United Methodist Church, dating from 1862 and located at the southern end of town on Main Street. The Brignole Building on Main is the oldest and largest building in town, dating from 1859 and featuring extensive use of stone; the Bellotti Inn, built in 1863, still operates as a hotel and restaurant, boasting period decor in its guest rooms; and the charming wood-frame Sutter Creek Inn, which dates from 1859 and is the former home of California Senator E.C. Voorhies, has "swinging beds" in many of its rooms, suspended from the ceiling by means of chains. Several other historic structures of note can also be seen in town, especially on Main Street which is filled with restored old buildings housing antique shops and quaint restaurants.

Above Main Street, at the northern approach to Sutter Creek is the site of the old Lincoln Mine, once owned by Leland Stanford, founder

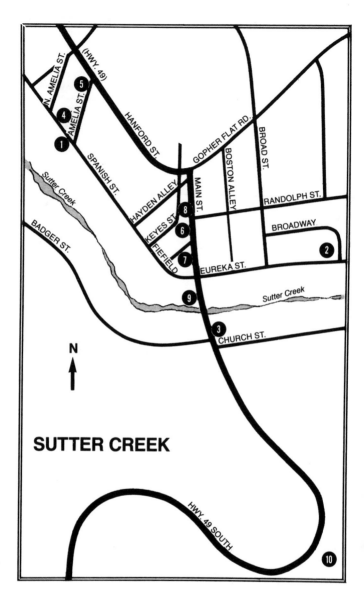

SUTTER CREEK

Points of Interest -
1) Downs' Mansion
2) Knight's Foundry (c.1873)
3) United Methodist Church
   (1862)
4) Immaculate Conception
   Church

5) Trinity Episcopal Church
6) Brignole Bldg. (1859)
7) Bellotti Inn (1863)
8) Sutter Creek Inn (1859)
9) R.C. Downs Museum
10) Old Eureka Mine

of Stanford University and Governor of California. Just below the mine site on Amelia Street are two quite interesting churches, the Trinity Episcopal Church and the Church of Immaculate Conception, both with their intricate Victorian details and some ancient and beautiful stained glass.

Spanish Street, which intersects Amelia a block or so to the west, just to the back of Main Street, has a row of splendid period homes, the loveliest of which is the Downs Mansion, with its southern elegance and bunched up bushes and trees, once the home of Robert Downs, foreman of the Lincoln Mine. Be sure also to visit the R.C. Downs Museum, housed in the Pasty Place, just over the creek, off Main Street. It has a good collection of mining machinery and old tools and photographs, and at the Pasty Place one can sample authentic Cornish pasties and local, Shenandoah wines.

Another attraction at Sutter Creek, of quite a different sort, is the historic Knight's Foundry, which dates from 1873 and is probably the only water-powered foundry in the United States today. It is powered by a 42-inch water wheel, and around noon on Fridays you can watch molten metal being poured into cast dyes, reminiscent of the old days when the foundry was casting metal wheels and mining machinery for California's mines. More recently, the foundry cast pilasters for the restoration of the State Capitol.

Just south of Sutter Creek lies Sutter Hill, with its assortment of shops and commercial establishments, and east of there on Ridge Road (Highway 104) can be seen the headframe of the famous Central Eureka Mine, the richest mine in the region, which produced an estimated $36 million in gold between 1860 and 1958. The mine was originally developed by Alvinza Hayward, California's first mining millionaire. A little farther on the same road is the site of the Old Eureka Mine, once owned by Hetty Green, of Wall Street fame, reputedly the richest woman in the world in her time.

Jackson

Three miles or so south of Sutter Creek and we are at Jackson, which, besides being the county seat and the largest town in the county, is home to the famous Kennedy Tailing Wheels — which have the distinction of being the most photographed relics in the Mother Lode. The wheels can be seen at the Kennedy Wheels Park on Jackson Gate Road, just to the north of Jackson. There were originally four wheels, each 58 feet in diameter, but two have fallen since and now lie in a state of ruin. Built in 1912 after a new federal law went into effect requiring that all mine tailings be impounded, the wheels removed some 850 tons of gravel every 24 hours from the watershed of the Jackson Creek just below the mine, and transported them over two hills to an impound tank farther east; each successive wheel lifted the gravels 42 feet and deposited them into a gravity flume, which then carried the wastes to the next wheel along. From the hill upon which Wheel No. 1 is located, you can see the Kennedy Mine headframe in the distance, built over a vertical shaft that reaches over a mile deep;

guided tours of the mine buildings and headframe are conducted once a year, usually in late spring or early fall (See *Mine Tours* in the practical information). The Kennedy Wheels Park also has some good picnicking possibilities, and meandering foot-trails.

Below the park is the small but lovely St Sava's Serbian Orthodox Church, which displays a rather unusual architectural style and is indeed quite photogenic. This is the mother church for the order in North America, and surrounding it is a cemetery of some interest. Both the church and cemetery date from 1894.

Also near to the Kennedy Mine, and well worth visiting, is the Argonaut Mine, reached on Argonaut Lane, west off the highway. The Argonaut operated for over half a century, and in 1922 it was the scene of one of California's worst mining tragedies, when 47 miners became trapped, and died, in a mine fire. The mine's mighty headframe can be seen on the slope of a hill, built over an inclined shaft with a depth of 6,300 feet.

Jackson itself is a mixture of old and new. Much of the old town is nestled along a small section of Main Street, with a few of the old buildings scattered on the hill above, on Church and Court streets. The National Hotel at the head of Main Street, first built in 1849 and rebuilt in 1862 after a fire destroyed it as well as much of the original town earlier that year, dominates the present old town section; and as added interest, it is still in operation as a hotel and restaurant today — after well over 100 years. Nearby is the old I.O.O.F. Hall, dating from 1862 and believed to be the tallest three-story building in the United States; it once also housed the Wells Fargo offices which handled over $100 million in gold, in dust and bullion. Also of interest are the Masonic Hall on Broadway, built in 1854 and acknowledged as one of the oldest downtown buildings; and the old drug store on Main Street, dating from 1855, which once housed the respected *Amador Dispatch*, and where, after the assassination of Lincoln, the newspaper's secessionist publisher and editorialist were arrested and conveyed to Alcatraz. Several other historic buildings, and some plaques of much interest, can also be found on Main and some of the adjoining streets.

The hill above Main Street is also quite rewarding. Church Street of course has its delightful churches, the United Methodist Church and St. Patrick's Catholic Church, dating from 1869 and 1868, respectively; and on Court Street is the former home of U.S. Senator James T. Farley, originally built in 1860, which also served as storage for county records during the 1862 fire. A special place to visit here, however, at the far end of Church Street, is the old Brown House, one of the oldest residences in Jackson, dating from 1854. In the 1920s, it provided the setting for the movie, *Boys Will Be Boys*, starring Will Rogers. It now houses the Amador County Museum, where displays include mining artifacts and rooms decorated in 19th century splendor. Be sure to take the guided tour which will show you working scale models of a Kennedy Tailing Wheel and a stamp mill that actually crushes small rocks into sand. On the museum grounds are displays of some large pieces of mining equipment, and an interesting model of a 56-foot narrow-gauge steam locomotive which starred as the "Hooterville Cannonball" in the TV series, *Petticoat Junction*.

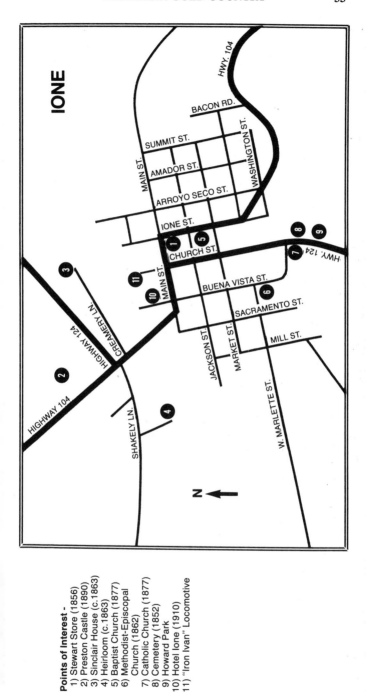

IONE

Points of Interest -
1) Stewart Store (1856)
2) Preston Castle (1890)
3) Sinclair House (c.1863)
4) Heirloom (c.1863)
5) Baptist Church (1877)
6) Methodist-Episcopal
   Church (1862)
7) Catholic Church (1877)
8) Cemetery (1852)
9) Howard Park
10) Hotel Ione (1910)
11) "Iron Ivan" Locomotive

Also take the time to tour Camanche Lake, which lies farther south from Buena Vista. Camanche is one of the finest lakes in the region, with roughly 62 miles of shoreline to enjoy. It has two independent resorts, one each on the north and south shores, and facilities include camping, picnicking, hiking, horseback riding, boating, fishing, swimming, and even some worthwhile beaches and a waterslide. During holiday weekends the lake is especially popular.

East to Pine Grove and the Indian Grinding Rock

From Jackson it is roughly 9 miles east on Highway 88 to Pine Grove, a town almost the size of Jackson, but with a distinct mountain flavor. On the highway here is the old Pine Grove Hotel, itself more than a hundred years old, but which stands on the site of the original Pine Grove House, built in 1855, for which the town is named. Also of interest are the old schoolhouse with its bell-tower, dating from 1869; the Pine Grove Town Hall, built in 1879; the Pine Grove Community Church on Church Street, and, beside it, an historic cemetery that dates from 1860. Pine Grove also has a worthwhile park which was created by a grant in 1870.

One and one-half miles north of Pine Grove on the Pine Grove-Volcano Road is *Chaw'Se*, or the Indian Grinding Rock State Historic Park. This is the only park of its kind in the state, centered around the Miwok Indian culture, with a real Miwok village, a ceremonial roundhouse, and a cultural center which has displays of Indian baskets, weavings, jewelry, and tools. But without doubt the showpiece of the park is the great Indian Grinding Rock, the largest of its kind yet found in America, a replica of which is on display at the Smithsonian Institute in Washington, D.C. The rock is pitted with 1,185 mortar holes which were once used by Miwok women to grind acorns and nuts and seeds into palatable food; also to be seen on the rock are some 365 petroglyph designs. The park has good picnicking and camping facilities, and in September each year, usually during the last weekend, the Miwok people gather here to celebrate their "Big Time," a festivity featuring tribal dances, traditional Indian hand-games, and bartering of native handiworks.

Volcano

Four beautiful country roads descend on Volcano, each with its own dramatic approach, from Sutter Creek, Pine Grove, Pioneer, and one from the Daffodil and Observatory hills just to the north. The last of these is of course the most spectacular, offering fine mountain scenery along its steep descent; but the road from Pine Grove and, consequently, the Indian Grinding Rock State Park, has an added attraction: a little way before Volcano a small side road leads to the Masonic Caves, which comprise a series of three or four limestone caverns, in the largest of which, in 1853, the Masonic brethren held three successive meetings prior to building the Masonic Lodge at nearby Volcano. The caves are open to the public for viewing.

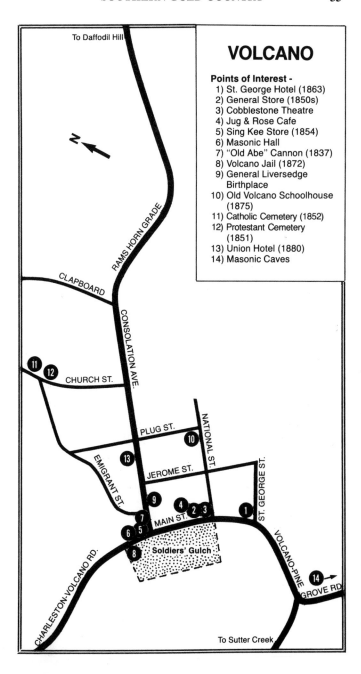

VOLCANO

Points of Interest -
1) St. George Hotel (1863)
2) General Store (1850s)
3) Cobblestone Theatre
4) Jug & Rose Cafe
5) Sing Kee Store (1854)
6) Masonic Hall
7) "Old Abe" Cannon (1837)
8) Volcano Jail (1872)
9) General Liversedge Birthplace
10) Old Volcano Schoolhouse (1875)
11) Catholic Cemetery (1852)
12) Protestant Cemetery (1851)
13) Union Hotel (1880)
14) Masonic Caves

It must be right to say that Volcano — named for its unique setting in a bowl-shaped valley which early day miners once thought to be the crater of a volcano — is the most picturesque town in the Mother Lode, with its surrounding pine-clad mountains and its neat, tree-lined streets upon which are some very attractive dressed-stone buildings and frame cottages. Main Street has its own superb collection of native stone buildings; the old General Store, built in 1852 and said to be in continuous operation since; the Cobblestone Theatre, originally built in the 1850s and rebuilt in the 1960s, where the Volcano Pioneers Theatre Group now performs; the Jug & Rose Cafe, built in 1954 with stones taken from the ancient ruins of another store at a nearby gold camp; and, farther on, at the west end of Main stands the two-story Sing Kee Store, with iron shutters and gray, native stone walls, built in 1854. Also on Main is the old Assay Office, a frame structure dating from 1871, and on the south side of the street is the Soldiers Gulch (park), where the ground falls away along a splendid grass-covered slope that was created in the 1890s by hydraulic sluicing.

Other places of interest at Volcano include the venerable St. George Hotel, a three-story wood-frame hostelry dating from 1863, which is still in use; the Old Brewery, featuring stone construction; the Masonic Hall, built in about 1856; the wood-frame Union Hotel, dating from 1880 and now a private residence; the old schoolhouse, crowned with a bell-tower, which was in use as a school from 1870 to 1955; and the Volcano Jailhouse, built from stone in 1872, and said to be escape-proof. Some other old buildings can been seen at random too, and two historic cemeteries lie just to the northwest of town — the Catholic cemetery and the Protestant Cemetery, dating from 1852 and 1851, respectively.

Volcano's greatest glory, however, is "Old Abe" (and few would argue otherwise) — a 6-pounder bronze cannon, cast in Massachusetts in 1837 and said to be the oldest such cannon in America. It was brought to Volcano by Union supporters during the Civil War, in 1862, to squelch a Confederate uprising. Rebel control of the town, we are told, would have meant diversion of its gold to the Southern cause — and Volcano was rich, with its gold output estimated to be in excess of $90 million. The uprising, needless to say, was put down, without firing a shot, and the cannon can now be seen in its shed just to the north of the Sing Kee Store on Consolation Avenue.

Take the time also to visit the birthplace of General Liversedge (of Iwo Jima fame) on Consolation Avenue, near Emigrant Street. For those who can remember, it was Liversedge's Marine unit that first raised the American Flag on Mount Suribachi, Iwo Jima, during World War II.

Daffodil Hill

Volcano has yet another surprise to delight the visitor. Daffodil Hill, a 4-acre ranch lying just above Volcano on Ram's Horn Grade, has one of the most astonishing displays of spring color anywhere, well worth a visit if you happen to be there in season. For roughly six weeks each year, usually from about mid-March until the end of April, the entire hillside is transformed into a flower garden of irresistible natural beauty, with over 500,000 daffodils and other flowers in bloom. There are at least 300 varieties of daffodils here, most common among which are the large yellow King Alfreds and the lovely white Mountain Hoods, and several hyacinths, crocus, tulips, violets and lilacs can also be seen scattered around in an assortment of pottery. Old wagons and pieces of antiquated farm machinery lie about near weathered structures, and often enough peacocks and other wild fowl can be seen upon the grounds, hopping and strutting among the flowers. You can wander down narrow, enchanting foot-trails that meander through the gardens for closer viewing, and there is also a delightful picnic area by the entrance. The hill opens to the public when 25% or more of the flowers are in bloom, and closes when only 25% remain.

A mile or so west of Daffodil Hill is Observatory Point, where a plaque marks the site of California's first amateur astronomical observatory of record. It was from here that George Madeira discovered the great comet of 1861, using a 3-inch refractor telescope.

THE ANGELS CAMP AREA

The Mokelumne River flows along the northern border of the Calaveras (Spanish for "skulls") County, separating it from the Amador County — Jackson area — to the north. This, then, is one of California's original 27 counties, established in early 1850. It is notable mainly as the "jumping frog" county, made famous by Mark Twain's classic tale, "The Celebrated Jumping Frog of Calaveras County." The major county town here is Angels Camp, besides which there are the less important but equally interesting communities of San Andreas — which also happens to be the county seat — and Murphys, Copperopolis, and Mokelumne Hill, the northernmost.

Mokelumne Hill

It is almost impossible to see Mokelumne Hill from the highway, driving south on 49, which really makes it all the more appealing, and a favorite with holiday-makers. Take the "historic" detour east off the highway; it will lead you directly to the town's small but enchanting Main Street, which has some fine old buildings on it, and off to the side of which a half dozen or so tiny, twisty streets, beautifully shaded by locusts and oaks, go dancing down the hillside into the essentially domestic parts, with thick blackberry bushes to be encountered near the bottom, ripe for picking in the summer months.

Mokelumne Hill is dominated by its steepled wooden church, dating from 1856, and its iron-shuttered stone I.O.O.F. Hall which has the distinction of being the oldest three-story structure in the Gold Country. The Hotel Leger on Main Street, however, is one of the finest buildings here, originally built in the 1860s and recently restored to its former glory. Just to the back of the hotel is the site of an arena where bear and bull fights were staged for miners' entertainment. Also worth visiting is the Keskydee shop and art gallery, housed in an historic stone building directly across from the hotel, and containing some remarkable antiques and original paintings displayed in a primitive gallery setting. Some other old buildings, mostly built from locally quarried rhyolite tuff, and two or three frame cottages can be seen here too.

Mokelumne Hill also has a rich history. It was once a principal mining town of California, and the seat of Calaveras County from 1855 to 1865. Gold was first discovered here in 1848, and the placer diggings were found to be so rich that claims were restricted to 16-foot squares: nearby Corral Flat alone produced in excess of $30 million in gold, and Happy Valley, also close by, was almost as rich. In 1850, the *Calaveras Chronicle*, one of the earliest newspapers in the Mother Lode, was established here. Also, during the 1850s, Joaquin Murrieta, legendary bandit of the Gold Country, is said to have headquartered here, and in 1851, a "French War" was fought on nearby French Hill, in which American miners drove off a group of Frenchmen from a particularly rich claim. On the grisly side, Mokelumne Hill experienced a period of some 17 weeks when a murder was committed every week, and on one weekend, five people were killed.

A worthwhile detour from Mokelumne Hill, roughly 12 miles east on Highway 26, is West Point, a modest vacation-home community with a few old buildings and with associations to Kit Carson and Bret Harte. It was once a gold mining town, but was named earlier for the fact that this was the westernmost point reached by Kit Carson during his search for a pass over the Sierra in 1844, due to the high waters of the Mokelumne River.

Happy Valley, which has an ancient stone structure, and Glencoe and Wilseyville, all lie on the way to West Point, and just to the south, off on a side road that branches from Highway 26, is Rail Road Flat which also witnessed some years of mining activity during the 1850s.

Paloma, another old mining camp which is now an historical landmark, is 4 miles west of Mokelumne Hill on Highway 26. The Gwin Mine, which operated there from 1883 to 1908, produced an estimated $7 million in gold. Just south of Paloma, also of interest, is Double Springs; it has one or two historic relics.

San Andreas

Not far from Mokelumne Hill, to the south, is San Andreas, spoiled by the highway in some ways, but which nevertheless has a small section of its old Main Street where one can search out two or three quite splendid dressed-stone buildings, dating from the 1800s. The small Fricot Building, for one, erected in 1851, now houses the county library; and near to it is the old, two-story Courthouse & Archives Building (formerly the Hall of Records and I.O.O.F. Hall), dating from 1896, which, besides housing the county courthouse and archives office, has a museum, an historical society office, an old jail, a law library, and until recently it was even home to the Calaveras County Chamber of Commerce. The museum on the second floor has a series of displays depicting pioneer 19th-century life in the Mother Lode, including a miner's cabin, a general store, an early Mother Lode Catholic Church, and a wealth of artifacts, old photographs and mining exhibits. Also of interest is the jailhouse at the back of the building, which has a "jail cell" exhibit, said to be the cell in which slept Black Bart (also known as Charles Bolton), the self-styled poet and highwayman who held up 28 stagecoaches with an unloaded gun, and always said "please" when robbing them. Black Bart awaited trial here after his capture in 1883, and the much-publicized trial was held in the courtroom directly above.

Nearby, on the highway one can see the beautifully restored frame home of Sheriff Ben Thorn, the lawman who brought about the capture of Black Bart. The Thorn Mansion, dating from 1861, is set on three lovely acres, with lush gardens and waterfalls and some worthwhile views. It is now a bed and breakfast inn, open to the public for lodging.

San Andreas has other good accommodations as well, plus some fine restaurants and modern shops. There is also a modest-size airfield just out from town, and west off the highway lies a cemetery of historic interest, where the oldest grave dates from 1851.

For a side trip from San Andreas, try the Railroad Flat Road (which goes off Highway 49) east to Mountain Ranch, a distance of some 9 miles. At the very outset, a short detour to the south off the Railroad Flat Road will lead you to Calaveritas, which has some gold rush buildings and its associations with the legendary Joaquin Murrieta. The strange thing about Joaquin Murrieta, however, is that no one is quite certain whether he was just a character from a legend, or whether he really did exist. In any case, Murrieta, it is said had tunnels all over California, into which he would disappear, like a jackrabbit into a burrow, when fleeing from the law; until in 1853 he was shot and killed by a bounty hunter and his head was then cut off and pickled in a jar of alcohol, for all to see.

Farther on, another little detour south off Railroad Flat Road will bring you to Cave City, near to which are some interesting limestone caverns where several chambers and passages, filled with fascinating stalagmite-stalactite formations, can be explored. The caves were once visited by writers Mark Twain and Bret Harte, and renowned naturalist John Muir who wrote of them in his book, *Mountains of California*.

Finally, there is Mountain Ranch, with its ancient Domenghini Store and one or two other stone and wood-frame buildings, as well as several assorted relics from the gold rush era.

The Jenny Lind Detour

Westward from San Andreas on Highway 12 lies Valley Springs, important mainly for its superb location at the crossroads of Highways 26 and 12, with two or three smaller country roads radiating out from it as well. Near to it is the New Hogan Reservoir, a year-round public recreation area, reached on a small side road off Highway 12. And north of Valley Springs, some 3 miles distant, is Campo Seco, which also is to be recommended as a side trip; it has several photogenic ruins and two cemeteries of historic interest.

From Valley Springs you can follow Highway 26 southwest through some mild countryside, remembering to turn south onto Milton Road, about 6 miles down. From the turnoff it is only a mile or so to Jenny Lind, which sits directly above the Calaveras River and which has some old frame homes, the ruins of an adobe store, and a notable I.O.O.F. Hall worth investigating. But of even greater interest is the stark landscape encountered just to the south of Jenny Lind, where rows upon rows of dredging waste piles cover the ground for many miles around, creating a sight of quite a different sort. These, however, are the remains of the feverish dredging activity that once gripped Jenny Lind, beginning in 1902 and lasting several years.

From Jenny Lind one can either drive south to Milton and Copperopolis (described in a later section), and so to Angels Camp, or return to San Andreas via Valley Springs and proceed south on our main artery, Highway 49.

South to Angels Camp

It is an easy, 15-mile drive from San Andreas to Angels Camp south on Highway 49. But first, above Angels Camp there is Altaville, which in 1972 was incorporated into the former, making the main street of Angels Camp all of 4 miles long. Altaville itself has some fine old buildings to interest the visitor: the red-brick Altaville Grammar School, dating from 1858 and said to be the oldest grammar school in California; the Prince & Garibardi Store, a two-story stone building with iron shutters and ornate balcony rails, dating from 1852; and the historic Altaville Foundry (now the California Electric Steel Company), which has been in continuous operation since 1854, manufacturing mining equipment and machinery of sorts. West off the highway are three historic cemeteries worth investigating, all quite close together; the Serbian Cemetery dates from 1910, and the Protestant and Catholic cemeteries go back to 1855.

Angels Camp, of course, is indelibly associated with Mark Twain's classic tale of "The Celebrated Jumping Frog of Calaveras County." In fact, the town's greatest attraction is its Jumping Frog Jubilee, held each May at the county fairgrounds at nearby Frogtown, just to the south. This is one of the premier frog jumping contests of the world, which draws contestants and spectators by the thousand, often including a celebrity or two. Frogs can be rented locally (that is if you don't already have a pet frog), and it is a competition to judge which frog jumps farthest in three consecutive jumps. The event's main attraction, however, must at least in part rest with the contestants, who do all sorts of strange things to inspire and incite their entries, vying for that cherished first-prize.

Angels Camp has many ancient and lovely buildings in its rather well-preserved old town, some more impressive than others. The Angels Hotel, where Mark Twain originally heard the tale of the jumping frog, stands at the south end of Main Street, with a frog monument directly in front of it; it dates from 1855. At the other end of the downtown section is the Peirano Building, with its sturdy rock walls and iron doors, built in 1854 and said to have survived three major fires. Also, somewhere in the center of Main Street are the Stickle Brothers' stores, two fine examples of native stone construction, dating from 1856 and 1860. Several other historic buildings and restored

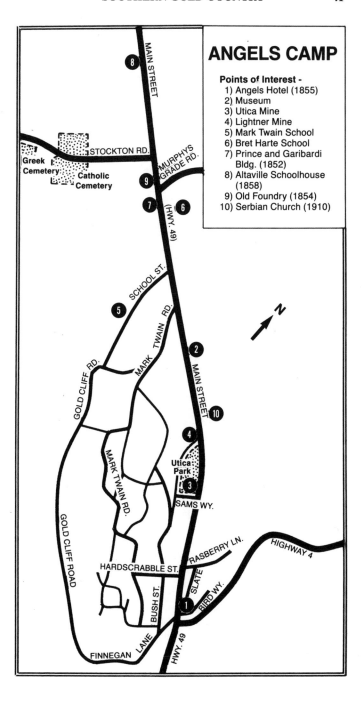

ANGELS CAMP

Points of Interest -
1) Angels Hotel (1855)
2) Museum
3) Utica Mine
4) Lightner Mine
5) Mark Twain School
6) Bret Harte School
7) Prince and Garibardi Bldg. (1852)
8) Altaville Schoolhouse (1858)
9) Old Foundry (1854)
10) Serbian Church (1910)

homes can also be seen on Main and some of the adjoining side streets.

North of the old town stands the glorious St. Vasilije's Serbian Orthodox Church, the second oldest Serbian church in the United States, built in 1910. Farther still is the City of Angels Museum, where displays include mining artifacts, pioneer household items, antique guns and knives, early Jumping Frog Jubilee souvenirs, ore samples, and a working scale model of a stamp mill. On the museum grounds outside are to be found drill cores from local mines, some antique carriages, a steam locomotive from the Jamestown-Angels Camp Railroad which operated here from 1902 to 1935, and a few pieces of heavy mining equipment.

Angels Camp also has a notable mining past. Five sizeable mines — the Utica, Lightner, Angels, Stickle and Sultana — were located right on Main Street in Angels Camp, and between 1886 and 1910 they produced a combined total of around $20 million in gold. At the site of the Utica there is now a park, which was built in 1954; the main shaft of the mine can still be seen in the park, cemented over, and many of the other shafts of the mine have been filled to a 60-foot level, after numerous cave-ins resulted in ground slippage, lowering the park level to several feet below the highway onto which it fronts. The park has a children's playground and some good picnicking possibilities. The statue in the park is that of Mark Twain, gifted to the city in 1945 by a motion picture company making a film on the life of Twain, starring Frederick March. Adjoining to the north of Utica Park is the site of the Lightner Mine, where a display of mining machinery, taken from the Lightner, can be viewed. North still are the sites of the Angels, Stickle and Sultana mines, though without plaques or markers to indicate these.

For a bit of mining lore, however, consider the story of how quartz gold was first discovered in Angels Camp. It is said that a man named Bennegar Rasberry somehow managed to get the muzzle-loader jammed in his gun, and. unable to release it manually, he fired it into the ground. The rod struck and split a stone, revealing what was unmistakably the glitter of gold. Rasberry took $10,000 in three days from his claim, then went on to reap a fortune following the vein, right on what is now downtown Main Street. How much truth there is to this, it is not quite certain, but local historians will tell you that no one could have invented a name like Bennegar Rasberry. In any event, there is a street in Angels Camp named after Rasberry.

Immediately south of Angels Camp on the highway (49) is to be found the two-story stone-brick Romaggi House, built in the 1850s and now partially in ruin, and 3 miles or so south of there is Carson Hill, honeycombed with many miles of underground mine workings, including a shaft that reaches some 5,000 feet deep. Carson Hill produced an estimated $26 million in gold, and some of the largest nuggets to be found in the Mother Lode were taken from here, including a record-size one that weighed 195 pounds! The area is now experiencing some renewed mining activity, sparked by the recent discovery of two new quartz veins. And who knows what this new bonanza will bring . . .

South again on 49, a little way from Carson Hill is the New Melones Reservoir, built on the Stanislaus River in the 1950s. The site of Melones (Spanish for "melons"), a former gold mining camp where gold nuggets the size of melon seeds were found during the early mining days, lies beneath the waters. The New Melones, however, has now blossomed into a year-round recreation area, quite popular with boaters, water-skiers, and anglers.

Murphys and Limestone Caverns

There are two prescribed routes between Angels Camp and Murphys: one over the old Murphys Grade, which is perhaps the shorter of the two; and the other by way of Highway 4, east. The second of these has one or two added attractions, like Vallecito (Spanish for "Little Valley"), some 5 miles distant, which has its Dinkelspiel Store, dating from the 1850s, and an ancient church bell on a stone monument. From Vallecito you can follow Parrots Ferry Road south a mile or so to the strange natural phenomenon of the Moaning Cave, which claims to be the largest public cavern in California — large enough to hold the Statue of Liberty upright and still have room to spare. Countless stalagmite-stalactite formations, of every shape, size and description, can be explored in the cave, and in its main chamber one can also view the 13,000-year-old remains of prehistoric people who fell to their deaths into the great cave in times immemorable; these are thought to be the oldest human remains yet found in North America. Tours are conducted through the cavern year-round, and for adventure hounds there is a unique and daring entry into the cave, rappelling 180 feet directly into the main chamber.

East from Vallecito on Highway 4 once more and we come to Douglas Flat, which has an old schoolhouse set on a hill above town, and a stone-adobe structure that once was a store-cum-bank where large amounts of gold were kept in a vault in holding; a "shot-gun window," used by an armed guard stationed there can still be seen by the rear door of the store. The schoolhouse dates from 1854, and the store, 1851.

And so to Murphys, which has one of the loveliest main streets in the Mother Lode, delightfully shaded by tall locusts and lined with a dozen or so brick-front buildings, typical of the gold rush era. Murphys' finest treasure, however, is its hotel, originally built in 1856 and recently restored to its former elegance. In its infancy, it was host to a long line of notables, such as Ulysses S. Grant, Mark Twain, Horatio Alger, Henry Ward Beecher, Sir Thomas Lipton, J. Pierpont Morgan, and Charles Bolton (Black Bart), among others; their names can be found in the hotel's old guest register, and some of the hotel's original guest rooms are now named for these illustrious guests. Directly across from the hotel is the old Murphys Jail, consisting of a one-room stone cell. Interestingly, its very first occupant, we are told, was its builder.

Other buildings of note on Main Street include the Thorpe Bakery and the Stanghetti, Thompson, Segale, Compere and Travers Buildings, all dating from the 1850s and 1860s. The last of these, the Travers Building, now houses the Old Timers Museum, where displays are of relics of the gold mining days, including a superb antique gun collection and original gold rush documents. Near to the museum, on the

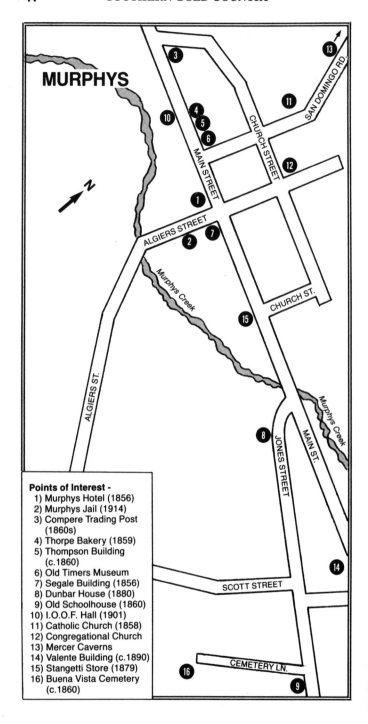

MURPHYS

Points of Interest -
1) Murphys Hotel (1856)
2) Murphys Jail (1914)
3) Compere Trading Post (1860s)
4) Thorpe Bakery (1859)
5) Thompson Building (c.1860)
6) Old Timers Museum
7) Segale Building (1856)
8) Dunbar House (1880)
9) Old Schoolhouse (1860)
10) I.O.O.F. Hall (1901)
11) Catholic Church (1858)
12) Congregational Church
13) Mercer Caverns
14) Valente Building (c.1890)
15) Stangetti Store (1879)
16) Buena Vista Cemetery (c.1860)

opposite side of the street, is the I.O.O.F. Hall, dating from 1901, and just above Main Street, on Church Street stands the small but impressive St. Patrick's Catholic Church, built in 1858 from locally baked clay bricks. There is an historic cemetery near the church.

On Jones Street, which goes off Main Street to emerge on the highway a little way down, one can search out some neat, well-kept homes, mostly dating from the 1800s. Noteworthy among these is the Dunbar House, dating from 1880 and now a charming bed and breakfast establishment. Also on Jones Street, quite close to the highway, is to be found Murphys' old schoolhouse, built in 1860 and in use until 1973. One of its graduates was Dr. Albert Michelson, America's first Nobel Prize winner in physics, in 1907, for his work in determining the velocity of light. The Chase House, where Michelson lived as a boy, can be seen on Church Street; it dates from 1862.

Murphys is also reputed to have been the starting point for Joaquin Murrieta, California's famous bandit; it has been said that it was here, in 1850, that Murrieta first joined the gang of the notorious Three-Fingered Jack and embarked on his murderous career.

Just outside Murphys on the San Domingo Road, which branches off Main Street near the Old Timers Museum and heads north, are the Mercer Caverns, originally opened to the public in 1887. A series of well-illuminated underground chambers and passages containing fascinating crystalline formations — stalagmites, stalactites, helictite, argonite, curtains, columns and flowstones — can be explored here. Some of the formations have taken such intriguing shapes as Angels Wings, an Organ Loft, Solomon's Thumb and a Chinese Meat Market. Guided tours of the caverns are conducted daily in summer, and on weekends in fall and winter.

From the caverns, the small, twisty road descends steeply into a pleasant little valley area, where one can visit the Stevenot Winery, one of the finest small wineries in the Mother Lode. It has a delightful picnic area, and a tasting room housed in a restored old barn. Some good apple wines are also available here.

Farther still, on the same road (which somewhere along the way becomes Sheep Ranch Road), is the tiny mountain village of Sheep Ranch, where George Hearst, U.S. Senator and father of press lord William Randolph Hearst, once had a gold mine.

Calaveras Big Trees

The Calaveras Big Trees State Park, 18 miles northeast of Murphys on Highway 4, is one of the most fascinating places of all to visit in the Sierra foothills. It comprises 5,994 acres of forestland, abundant in a variety of trees and plant-life, and containing mountain slopes, lava bluffs, a river canyon (that of the North Fork of the Stanislaus) and, best of all, two magnificent groves of *sequoiadendron giganteum* (giant sequoias) — the "Big Trees" — known to be the largest living things on earth. These last are indeed the most spectacular of all, the great glories of the park, dating from the Mesozoic Era — the age of the dinosaurs — and any effort is worth it to see these noble giants.

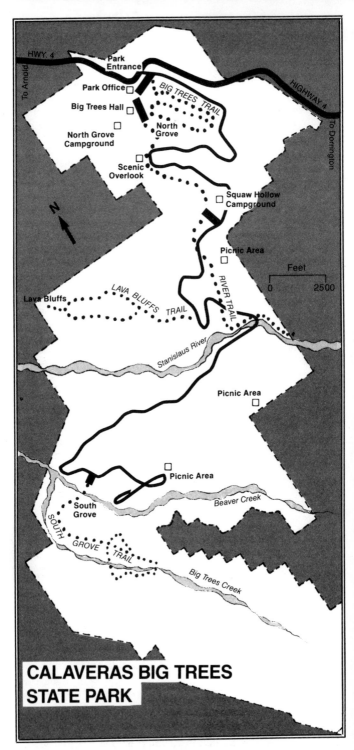

CALAVERAS BIG TREES STATE PARK

SONORA AND COLUMBIA

South of the New Melones Reservoir, Tuolumne — pronounced *Too-Ah-Le-Me* — County begins. Sonora and Columbia are the two principal county towns here; and the area takes in, besides, the townships of Chinese Camp, Jamestown, Big Oak Flat and Groveland.

In and Around Columbia

No tour of the Gold Country would be complete without a visit to Columbia, the "Gem of the Southern Mines," which produced in excess of $87 million in gold from a one-square-mile area. But before reaching Columbia, there are two small stops we must make. The first is Jackass Hill, itself reached on a small, steep side road off Highway 49, which has a reconstructed cabin in which Mark Twain and Bret Harte lived for several months, at different times, and where Twain in fact wrote his famous tale of "The Celebrated Jumping Frog of Calaveras County," from notes made earlier at Angels Hotel. The hill, of course, is named for the hundreds of traders' jackasses which, while resting there for the night enroute to the mines with supplies, brayed in concert. Directly below Jackass Hill is Tuttletown, essentially a wide spot on the highway but which nevertheless has the remains of an ancient stone store where Bret Harte once worked as a clerk.

Columbia lies a mile or so off Highway 49 on Parrots Ferry Road, just to the north of Sonora. The town is now part of a 273-acre state historic park, and it can be said that this is the best-preserved of all the Mother Lode towns, where one can truly recapture the atmosphere of the gold rush days. It has splendid, tree-shaded streets, lined with 1850s frame cottages and iron-shuttered brick buildings, some painstakingly restored, others quite artfully reconstructed to duplicate the original structures. Most of these old buildings now house gift and antique shops, specialty stores and quaint restaurants, while some continue to be private residences; and people live and work here, much like in the old days. Motor traffic is banned from many of the town's streets, which really makes it all the more attractive, given to leisurely exploring on foot. And to enhance all of this, some ancient and lovely gardens are being restored, notably a Nineteenth Century Rose Garden which features rose bushes from the 1830-1930 period, and an Irish Cottage Garden which has a variety of historic flowers and vegetables, originally grown by the Irish families that settled in Columbia during the gold rush.

The highlight of any visit to Columbia would have to be a ride on the Columbia Stagecoach — an authentic Abbott & Downing Concord Coach, built in 1874 — which will take you on some of Columbia's old back-country trails, and through the nearby Matelot Gulch where people still pan for gold. At the Wells Fargo Express Building, which also serves as the stagecoach office, there are some old scales on display, on which was weighed an estimated $55 million worth of

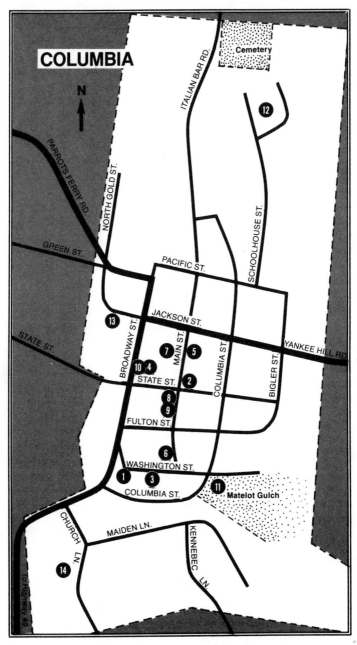

COLUMBIA

N

Cemetery

ITALIAN BAR RD.

PARROTS FERRY RD.

NORTH GOLD ST.

SCHOOLHOUSE ST.

GREEN ST.

PACIFIC ST.

JACKSON ST.

STATE ST.

BROADWAY ST.

MAIN ST.

COLUMBIA ST.

BIGLER ST.

YANKEE HILL RD.

STATE ST.

FULTON ST.

WASHINGTON ST.

COLUMBIA ST.

Matelot Gulch

CHURCH LN.

MAIDEN LN.

KENNEBEC LN.

to Highway 49

Points of Interest -
1) Fallon House Theatre
2) Museum
3) Columbia Gazette Museum
4) Firehouse No. 1
5) Firehouse No. 2
6) Wells Fargo Bldg.
7) City Hotel
8) Columbia House
9) Justice Court
10) I.O.O.F. Hall
11) Tent City
12) Schoolhouse
13) Church of the 49ers
14) St. Anne's Church

50

gold. In town are also two museums well worth visiting: the William Cavalier Museum has displays of 19th-century relics, including mining artifacts and pioneer household items; and the Columbia Gazzette Museum, which is housed in the old newspaper building (circa 1853), has antique printing presses and other 1800s printing equipment, as well as an historic bookshop, and an excellent recount of the history of journalism in California. Several other exhibits of historical interest can be randomly explored throughout town, among them an early-day drug store, an old-fashioned dental clinic, and an historic courtroom which is still in use, said to be the oldest courtroom in continuous use in the county. Also, here are two red-brick firehouses to delight the visitor, with beautifully-restored antique fire-fighting equipment on display; of special note is a little two-cylinder hand-pumper, the *Papeete*, with leather hoses and buckets, seen at Firehouse No. 1.

Columbia has many other attractions and fine old buildings to interest visitors. One can search out the historic St. Anne's Catholic Church, for instance, which stands on a hill above town, with its parish cemetery to be seen on the hillside just below; the church dates from 1856 and is believed to be the oldest brick Catholic church in California. Another quite splendid church, the Church of the 49ers, is located at the western end of town; this is thought to be the oldest Presybeterian church in use in the state, rebuilt in 1950, after being destroyed by fire, as an exact replica of the original. The old Columbia Schoolhouse to the north of town, dating from 1860, is also not without its dinstinction; it is said to be one of the first public schools in the state. Of interest, too, is the venerable City Hotel, originally built in 1857 and restored in 1974; it is now operated by students from nearby Columbia College, and the restaurant here is much to be recommended for its superb French cuisine. You should find the time also to visit Columbia's historic Fallon House Theatre, built in 1885 as an addition to the hotel of the same name, where reputable theater groups now perform in spring, summer and fall, offering some delicious comedy and old-fashioned melodrama.

Columbia is easily at its best in summer, when the streets here are dotted with lemonade carts, street fiddlers and amateur jugglers; and a "tent city," reminiscent of old gold rush camps, sprouts at nearby Matelot Gulch, with local merchants portraying 19th-century pioneers and bearded prospectors giving panning lessons to children. Quite close to here, a real quartz-gold mine, with a 700-foot horizontal tunnel, is also open to public tours.

Columbia also has a notable airport, open to commercial airlines, and air tours can be taken from there for some spectacular aerial sightseeing. Additionally, there are two excellent campground resorts nearby, the 49er Trailer Ranch and the Marble Quarry Resort; the latter of these has an historic marble quarry quite close to it, which supplied the marble used in several early-day San Francisco buildings.

A little way to the southeast of Columbia on Sawmill Flat Road a plaque marks the site of Sawmill Flat, an old mining and lumbering camp which reputedly was a hideout for the famous bandit Joaquin Murrieta. North of Columbia, however, a winding section of Parrots Ferry Road will bring you to the Parrots Ferry Bridge, the second of three bridges on the River Stanislaus, built at the north end of the New Melones Reservoir. This, incidentally, is also the deepest point on the reservoir, where the gorge drops some 200 feet below water level. At the far end of the bridge is the site of the actual ferry - a flat-bottomed cable-propelled ferry which operated here from 1860 to 1903, when it was finally replaced by a bridge.

Two other places of note, near to Columbia, are Springfield and Shaws Flat. The first of these, overgrown with untamed grass and situated at the intersection of the Springfield and Shaws Flat roads, was named for its many natural springs, to which miners carted their gold-bearing dirt for washing during the early mining days. Springfield now has a noteworthy trout farm, open to the public. Shaws Flat, south of Springfield on a road of the same name, has its associations with James Fair, the silver king of Comstock fame, who mined here, unsuccessfully, in his early years. Also of interest here are the remains of the Mississippi House (saloon) dating from 1850.

Sonora

Above the town of Sonora stands the beautiful St. James Episcopal Church, with its unique arched windows, accentuated with fine stained glass, and its magnificent spire. It was originally built in 1860, though the spire and west side of the church were rebuilt in 1868, following a fire. This is not the oldest building in town, but quite probably the most photographed. The hill on which the church stands is the Piety Hill, and 100 feet or so to the northwest of it is the site of the Big Bonanza Mine, believed to have been the richest pocket-mine in the Mother Lode.

The charming Queen Anne Victorian directly across from the church, with its gingerbread trim and picturesque turret, dating from 1896, is the Frank and Ora Morgan Mansion; it was formerly the home of noted local attorney Frank Street, and his wife Ada Bradford Street — descendant of the Massachusetts Bradford family who sailed to the New World on the *Mayflower*. The Bradford descendants, in fact, exerted great influence in Sonora. There is an important street named after them, and on Dodge Street in the old town, one can search out the rambling two-story home of S.S. Bradford, lumber tycoon and father of Ada Bradford. The home dates from the 1890s and has an especially notable steamboat-style porch. Another, the dome-topped Bradford Building, dating from 1903 and featuring brick construction and copper doors, can be seen on Washington Street, in the center of town.

Sonora has other fine buildings, but the atmosphere is that of a busy city. Indeed, it is a place both ancient and important, and one of the most populous of the Mother Lode towns (second only to Placerville). The town is actually built in two sections: there is a downtown, which incorporates the old town; and a more modern section farther east on Washington Street, the town's main street, which sweeps down from Piety Hill on a southeast band several miles long. The old town lies directly beneath Piety Hill, and it is rich in restored 19th-century homes and historic buildings of various descriptions, some with covered walkways, yet others with modern facades. On Washington Street itself there are many old and lovely homes and historically interesting buildings, the finest — and oldest — of which is the Gunn House,

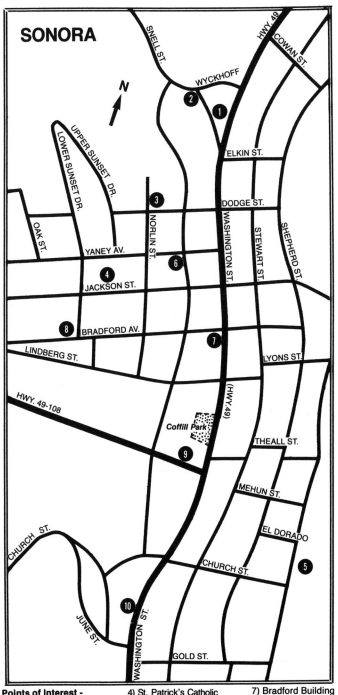

Points of Interest -
1) St. James Episcopal
   Church (1860)
2) Morgan Mansion (1896)
3) Bradford Home (1890s)

4) St. Patrick's Catholic
   Church (1863)
5) Sonora Grammar School
6) Tuolumne County
   Courthouse (1898)

7) Bradford Building
8) Tuolumne County
   Museum
9) Visitors Bureau
10) Gunn House (1850)

53

dating from 1850 and said to have once housed the first newspaper published in California's mining region. It is now a bed and breakfast inn of considerable repute, and tours can often be taken through it. Also visit Coffill Park on Washington, which is bordered by the Sonora Creek, and in which was found a 22-pound solid gold nugget during the early days of mining. The park has some picnicking opportunities.

More splendid, restored homes can be found on the adjoining Stewart Street and Bradford Avenue. The latter, of course, has a bonus. The old county jail, rebuilt in 1866 and now housing the Tuolumne County Museum, is located there; museum displays include items of local historical interest.

Take the time also to visit the impressive three-story Roman-pressed-brick County Courthouse on Yaney Avenue, which was built in 1898 at a cost of $105,000. It sits on the site of a former wood-frame courthouse building, erected in 1854. Opposite the courthouse is the more modern but equally impressive Albert N. Francisco Building; it occupies the site of the original Union Democrat Building, which housed the *Union Democrat* (1854-1954) — one of the Gold Country's oldest continuously published newspapers. Two other places of note are the Sonora Grammar School on Barretta Street, with its imposing columned facade, dating from 1909; and the steepled St. Patrick's Catholic Church on Jackson Street, dating from 1863, and quite lovely.

Sonora is also home to the Tuolumne County Fairgrounds, where many special events are held each year, and it has good accommodations and restaurants, and a profusion of modern shops and shopping centers with chain stores. There is even a local theater here, offering year-round performances.

Gold Camps and Resort Towns

If you continue southeast from Sonora on Washington Street, it will bring you out onto Highway 108, east, and some miles from Sonora, both on and off the highway, there are a handful of quite interesting small towns to be encountered. Standard and Tuolumne, two mining and lumbering camps, are reached on small side roads to the south off the highway. Each has plaques of historical interest and one or two relics from the gold rush days, and Tuolumne, formerly Summersville, is also home to the historic Westside & Cherry Valley Railway — an old logging railroad with steam engines, which was used for public tours during the late 1970s and early 1980s, but which is now closed. It is hoped that it will reopen to the public in the near future.

Two other gold camps, Cherokee and Soulsbyville, lie above Tuolumne. Soulsbyville is notable as the site of the Soulsby Mine, the first major quartz mine of the county, which produced $6.5 million in gold before closing in 1900.

Farther still, on Highway 108, is the resort town of Twain Harte, abundant in vacation homes and soaring evergreens, and with a distinct mountain flavor. It has some good accommodations and restaurants. It is also a fine shopping place, and has two worthwhile golf courses.

At Miwuk-Village, which is 5 miles from Twain Harte, there is yet another golf course, and a much liked lodge. And beyond, 13 miles distant and several feet higher, is Pinecrest, with a lake of modest proportions and a reputable ski area, Dodge Ridge.

Jamestown and South

On Highway 49 once more, a mile or so to the south of Sonora and we come to Jamestown, the oldest of the towns in the "Southern Mines," first established in 1848 by one Colonel George James, for whom it is named. Just out from town, a little way to the south meanders the historically important Woods Creek, in which was found a 75-pound solid gold nugget in August of 1848, which in fact sparked off the rush to the southern regions. More recently, in 1984, a "strike" of some importance was made in the center of town, when a repair crew excavated a damaged sewer-pipe and gold was found in the ground directly beneath it (right on Main Street!), setting off a mini gold rush all of its own, lasting several days.

Jamestown is attractive in a rugged sort of way, with an especially notable main street — small, but cluttered with ancient and lovely stone and wood-frame buildings, many with overhanging balconies and covered walkways — where the atmosphere is truly that of the Old West. Interesting buildings here include the venerable National Hotel, dating from 1852 and recently restored to its formal perfection; the rebuilt, yet charming, Willows Hotel; the two-story Jamestown Hotel, featuring brick construction; the old Emporium Building, with its gingerbread trim and ornate balcony rails; and the Royal Hotel (1922). Several other fine buildings can also be seen on the main street, and above Main, on Seco Street stands the splendid Methodist Church, with its quaint belfry, dating from 1852.

A little to the east from the center of town, on 5th Street, lies the 26-acre Railtown 1897 State Historic Park — the showpiece of Jamestown. It is of course a theme park, centered around an historic railroad consisting of turn-of-the-century steam locomotives and railcars, and a fully equipped roundhouse where old engines are still being repaired and maintained. Tours of the roundhouse are conducted daily during summer, and there is an old-fashioned dining car on the premises open to the public, as well as a small picnic area; rail excursions are offered on weekends (see *Historic Railroad Tours* in the practical information). Railtown is also quite popular with Hollywood movie producers; dozens of feature and TV films have been shot on location here, including such all-time favorites as *High Noon* (1952) starring Gary Cooper, *The Virginian* (1929), W.C. Fields' *My Little Chickadee* (1940), *Chattannoga Choo Choo* (1983), *The Gambler* (1983) starring Kenny Rogers, and TV's *Petticoat Junction*, the greatest.

South from Jamestown we have a choice of roads, both rewarding. On Highway 49, 4 miles along, is Chinese Camp, a slumbering, pale-washed village, overgrown with wild grass and tarweed, and rose bushes and the locust-like native Chinese "Trees-of-Heaven." The camp was named in the early days for its disproportionately large Chinese population, and in 1861 it was the scene of the first Tong War in the state, fought between the Sam Yap and Yan Woo tongs, in which hundreds of warriors participated, 4 were killed, 12 wounded, and 250 taken prisoner — by the local sheriff. Worth investigating here are two iron-shuttered brick buildings, the old Post Office and the Wells Fargo Express Building, dating from 1854 and 1898, respectively, and both located on the tiny, deserted main street, thick with deep-green foliage. Also see the St. Francis Xavier's Catholic Church on the highway, built in 1855 and restored in 1949.

Some miles below Chinese Camp, over the Don Pedro Reservoir upon which houseboating is quite popular, there is Moccasin, with its elaborate power plant and a fish hatchery that is open to the public for viewing.

Alternatively, from Jamestown you can follow Seco Street south onto the Jacksonville Road — a wild sort of back-country road — skirting the Don Pedro Reservoir to the east and passing through the delectable village of Stent, where there is an ancient cemetery. The Jacksonville Road re-emerges on Highway 49 just above the Moccasin Creek Power Plant.

In any case, a worthwhile detour from Moccasin is Big Oak Flat, 8 miles east on Highway 120. Big Oak Flat was formerly known as the Savage Diggings, named for James Savage, soldier, miner and trader, who mined here in the early days and who became the first white man to explore the Yosemite Valley when he entered there accidentally in 1850 while in pursuit of a group of hostile Indians. The town was renamed in later years for an enormous, 13-foot-wide oak tree that once stood in the center of town and fell over when miners dug up the earth around it, to a depth of some 5 feet, in search of gold. (Big Oak Flat, incidentally, produced an estimated $28 million in gold.) There are two 1850s stone and adobe buildings here, of interest to the visitor.

Not far from Big Oak Flat, 2 miles, is Groveland, formerly named Garrotte for the much-publicized hanging of a horse thief here in 1850. Groveland has an old firehouse, an equally old jailhouse, and the Iron Door Saloon which dates from 1852 and which claims the distinction of being the oldest saloon in continuous operation in California. In June each year, the town hosts the "Old West Days," a Western fanfare featuring a mock hanging.

THE MARIPOSA AREA

The landscape of the Mariposa area — an area made up largely of the Mariposa County, lying adjacent to the Yosemite National Park — is distinguished by its primitive hills and remote valleys. Mariposa, the town, is the seat of this county. The area also has in it Coulterville, Bear Valley, and Hornitos, a surprising ghost town.

Coulterville

Northernmost among Mariposa County's gold towns is Coulterville, situated at the intersection of Highways 49 and 132 and the ancient Greeley Hill Road. It once was important as the gateway to

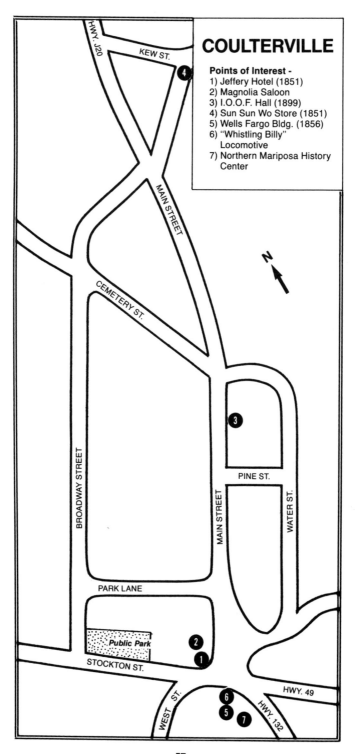

COULTERVILLE

Points of Interest -
1) Jeffery Hotel (1851)
2) Magnolia Saloon
3) I.O.O.F. Hall (1899)
4) Sun Sun Wo Store (1851)
5) Wells Fargo Bldg. (1856)
6) "Whistling Billy" Locomotive
7) Northern Mariposa History Center

HWY. J20
KEW ST.
MAIN STREET
N
CEMETERY ST.
BROADWAY STREET
MAIN STREET
PINE ST.
WATER ST.
PARK LANE
Public Park
STOCKTON ST.
HWY. 49
WEST ST.
HWY. 132

57

the Yosemite National Park — through much of the late 1800s and early 1900s — but its old and difficult road has since been superseded by the highway (120) just to the north.

Coulterville, more than any other mining town of its size, is bubbling over with history. It is a state historic landmark, and in 1981, its Main Street area was entered into the National Register of Historic Places, for all of the buildings on Main date from the 1800s and early 1900s, with the notable exception of one. There are, in fact, no less than 47 designated historic buildings (and sites) within Coulterville, and if we must be selective, we can choose the rock and adobe Jeffery Hotel, at the head of Main Street, as the grandest of them all. Originally built in 1851 as a Mexican fandango hall, with 3-foot-thick walls, it was converted into a hotel by an Englishman some years later, and in 1902, Theodore Roosevelt stayed here, enroute to Yosemite. The adjoining Magnolia Saloon is also not without historic merit: of special note are its bat-wing doors and authentic 1890s bar. The saloon is open to the public.

Directly across from the Jeffery Hotel, over the highway, stands the red-brick Wells Fargo Store, dating from 1856. It is said that Nelson Cody, brother of Buffalo Bill Cody, was once a clerk here. The delightful little steam locomotive at the front of the store is the *Whistling Billy*, brought over from the nearby Mary Harrison Mine; it once shuffled back and forth, between the mine and the stamp mills, along a 4-mile stretch of 30-inch gauge track that was known as "The Crookedest Railroad in the World." The tree beneath which the steam engine stands is the town's old Hanging Tree. Also of interest, near to the Wells Fargo Store, is the Northern Mariposa History Center, housed in the old, two-story brick Coulter Hotel, only part of which now remains; museum displays include mine photographs and 19th-century pioneer artifacts, centered around local history.

There are several other historically interesting buildings and fine pioneer homes throughout Coulterville, and at the far end of Main Street, to the north, one can visit the Sun Sun Wo Store, a small, charming adobe structure, dating from 1851; the original shelves and fixtures can still be seen within. Another point of interest is the old, neo-colonial Coulter House, dating from 1857 and located a little way to the northwest of the town center. This was once the home of George Coulter, one of the earliest residents of Coulterville, for whom the town is named.

Two cemeteries of historical interest can also be found on the outskirts of town, as well as the site of the third, the Old Chinese Cemetery, from where the deceased were removed and shipped back to mainland China.

Coulterville is also an ideal base from which to explore Lake McClure, a notable recreation area — lying just to the southwest — with an 18-hole golf course quite close to it. The lake has houseboat rentals.

South to Bear Valley

The stretch of country south of Coulterville borders on primitive and desolate, with dry, shrub-covered hills reaching deep into remote valleys and with the highway twisting and turning fiercely around these hills; until at Bagby (11 miles) we finally find the River Merced, the source of which are the great Yosemite Falls many miles to the east, but which here is at a mellow pace, reducing to a trickle by late summer. Bagby itself is only a site — of California's first power dam, and of pathfinder John Fremont's stamp mills. Some abandoned old mines can be seen on the Merced, upriver from Bagby.

South of Bagby is Bear Valley, notably associated with Fremont. Bear Valley, in fact, was the center of Fremont's 44,000-acre grant, upon which he spawned his vast mining empire. Interestingly, the grant was acquired for a sum of $3,000 in 1847, ratified by the Supreme Court in 1859, and sold by Fremont in 1863, for a reported $6 million. There are some picturesque ruins to be found here, and three or four historically interesting buildings, including the old Bon Ton Saloon which dates from 1860 and is now a restaurant, the Simpson & Trabucco Store, and the Oddfellows Hall, dating from 1852, and which for some years was the Oso Museum.

South still is Mount Bullion (6 miles), named for Fremont's father-in-law, Senator Thomas Hart Benton, who was also known as "Old Bullion" Benton, for his strong reliance on hard money — or bullion. There is an airfield at Mount Bullion.

The Hornitos-La Grange Loop

It is 13 miles from Bear Valley to Hornitos, journeying west on the Bear Valley Road (J-16), and here we are once again reminded of the Copperopolis countryside, with its shallow, rounded hills, dotted with gnarled blue oaks and strange dark-rock outcroppings. Hornitos itself lies in much the same surroundings. It is nevertheless one of the most surprising of all ghost towns you are likely to find in the Mother Lode. Once the rowdiest and most violent town in the West, with strong links to the notorious Joaquin Murrieta, it now sits in silence, with deserted streets and old, abandoned brick buildings, some with rusted iron shutters and doors. Of particular interest here are the Wells Fargo Building (1852), Masonic Lodge (1856), and the ruins of an adobe structure, dating from 1858, where D. Ghirardelli, of San Francisco chocolate fame, once operated a store. Also see the old, one-cell Hornitos Jail, with its 2-foot-thick granite walls, and the solitary St. Catherine's Catholic Church, set on a windswept hill above town, near to which there is an old fenced-off cemetery with strange tomb-like graves. Hornitos (Spanish for "little ovens") was actually named for these early graves, said to resemble little ovens.

Just out from Hornitos, westbound, we cross over the Merced River at Merced Falls, and here the Merced Falls Road branches north from the county road, J-16, and leads off toward the large, awkwardly-shaped Lake McClure, which has three different recreation areas, two of which are reached on this road, along small detours.

If we continue west from Merced Falls, however, there is Snelling (14 miles distant from Hornitos), an early ferry crossing, also on the Merced River. Snelling has some pleasant vistas and good fishing opportunities.

From Snelling go north, 11 miles, on the La Grange Road to the town of the same name, which sits astride the Tuolumne River, at the intersection of Highway 132. La Grange was also an early ferry crossing, which in the early 1900s witnessed four phases of mining — placer, tunneling, hydraulic and dredging. Among the historically interesting buildings in town are an I.O.O.F. Hall, the La Grange Hotel, the Levacci Building (1897), a wooden jailhouse (1858), and a native stone Trading Post, dating from 1850 and said to be the oldest stone building in town. An abandoned adobe building can be seen directly across from the stone Trading Post, built at about the same time. There is also a 12-cubic-foot dredge bucket display on the main street, believed to be one of the largest dredge buckets in the world. It once was used on a dredge operating in the area.

From La Grange it is roughly 25 miles east on Highway 132 — passing between the lakes Don Pedro and McClure — back to Coulterville, where we rejoin our main artery of travel, Highway 49. South from there and we are back at Bear Valley, then Mount Bullion, and so to Mariposa.

Mariposa

Mariposa, 11 miles south of Bear Valley on Highway 49, is also not without its associations with John Charles Fremont, the illustrious Western pioneer. In fact, Mariposa was once owned by Fremont, and some of the town's oldest streets are named for his family, such as Jessie, Charles, Bullion and Jones.

Mariposa is dominated by its lovely white frame church, set on a hill above town, to the south. This is the St. Joseph's Catholic Church, quite picturesque with its noble spire; it dates from 1861 and is said to have been in continuous use since it was first built. On the hillside to the back of the church one can explore the ruins of the locally famous Mariposa Mine, founded by Kit Carson, the noted scout, in 1848-1849. The mine produced an estimated $2 million in gold.

Below St. Joseph's lies Mariposa's old town, small but interesting. It is possible to walk around and explore the half-dozen or so historic buildings here, tucked away between more modern shops, one or two of which also feature covered walkways. Worth seeing are the iron-shuttered brick Trabucco Warehouse, which dates from previous to the 1866 fire that destroyed much of Mariposa; the old Schlageter Hotel, dating from 1859, where Presidents Grant and Garfield once stayed; the Christian Scientist Church, originally built in 1890 as a Methodist Church, and which is still in use; the I.O.O.F. Hall, 1867; and the Masonic Lodge, first built in 1853, destroyed by fire twice, and rebuilt for the final time in 1911. Also of interest, only a block or so from the main street, is the Old Jail, built in the 1860s from locally quarried granite — with walls 2½ feet thick. Two fine residences of historic note, the Trabucco House and the Jones House, are to be found farther to the north of the downtown section. The Trabucco House, home of Superior Court Judge Trabucco, dates from 1901, and the Jones residence, standing on a street of the same name and said to have once belonged to Fremont's brother-in-law, was built in 1858. This latter is the oldest residence in Mariposa.

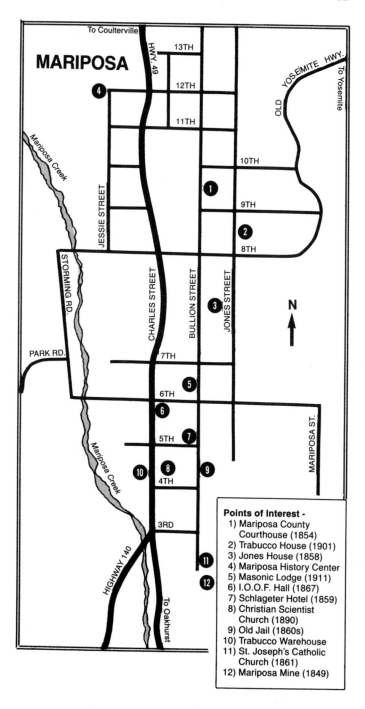

MARIPOSA

To Coulterville

HWY. 49

OLD YOSEMITE HWY.

To Yosemite

13TH
12TH
11TH
10TH
9TH
8TH
7TH
6TH
5TH
4TH
3RD

Mariposa Creek

JESSIE STREET

STORMING RD.

CHARLES STREET

BULLION STREET

JONES STREET

MARIPOSA ST.

PARK RD.

HIGHWAY 140

To Oakhurst

N

Points of Interest -
1) Mariposa County
   Courthouse (1854)
2) Trabucco House (1901)
3) Jones House (1858)
4) Mariposa History Center
5) Masonic Lodge (1911)
6) I.O.O.F. Hall (1867)
7) Schlageter Hotel (1859)
8) Christian Scientist
   Church (1890)
9) Old Jail (1860s)
10) Trabucco Warehouse
11) St. Joseph's Catholic
   Church (1861)
12) Mariposa Mine (1849)

The greatest glory of Mariposa yet, is its two-story wood-frame courthouse, set on splendid manicured grounds on a gentle hill on Bullion Street. It is acknowledged as the loveliest of all Gold Country buildings, and it may well be. It dates from 1854 (the clock on its tower dates from 1866), and has the distinction, also, of being the oldest courthouse in continuous use in the state, where court was held even before the Civil War. Although the courthouse is still in use, it is open to public viewing. Guided tours are conducted through it on weekends during the summer months, and you can see inside the old courtroom, where the ancient furnishings have remained unchanged in well over a century.

Another highlight of Mariposa is its History Center on Jessie Street (just off the main street), considered to be one of the most progressive small museums in the Mother Lode, where modern museum techniques are employed; displays are arranged by period and place, such as exhibits of the Ben Hur Ranch, Mary Harrison Mine, Hornitos General Store, Mrs. John Fremont's parlor, the 128-year-old *Mariposa Gazette*, and an 1800s schoolroom. On the museum grounds outside are several pieces of mining equipment, including a beautifully restored five-stamp mill, and a delightful Indian village, with real teepees.

Just south of Mariposa the motorist passes through the tiny, faded gold camps of Mormon Bar, Bootjack, Usona and Nipinnawasee. Between Usona and Nipinnawasee, one can see the old Chowchilla Schoolhouse from the highway; it dates from 1885.

THE OAKHURST AREA

The chief town of this area (which comprises the Eastern Madera County) is of course Oakhurst, itself lying some 25 miles south of Mariposa on Highway 49. Near to it are one or two resort areas such as Bass Lake and Fish Camp, and adjoining to the north of the Eastern Madera County is the spectacular Yosemite National Park.

Oakhurst and Around

Oakhurst is noted primarily for its flea markets and superb accommodations, and as a gateway to the Yosemite Valley for those traveling from the south. It is also, notably, the southern terminus of the Mother Lode Highway (Highway 49). The place to visit here is the Fresno Flats Historical Park, just out from the center of town on Road 427, where old structures, rescued from various places around, have been re-erected in a park-like setting. There are, for instance, two pioneer homes dating from the 1860s, an old wooden jail (circa 1880), the historic Fresno Flats School (1874), and one or two other ancient cabins. The old schoolhouse now contains a museum, where there are

slightly higher on holidays and weekends too.

Rates for accommodations, based on double occupancy, are categorized as follows: *Deluxe* (D), over $65; *Expensive* (E), $55-$65; *Moderate* (M), $40-$55; *Inexpensive* (I), under $40. (Note: rates are subject to change, and a sales tax will be added to your motel bill.)

Restaurant prices — based on a full course meal, excluding drinks, tax and tips — are categorized as follows: *Deluxe* (D), over $25; *Expensive* (E), $15-$25; *Moderate* (M), $10-$15; *Inexpensive* (I), under $10.

Most hotels and restaurants in the area accept major credit cards, but it is always worth inquiring beforehand.

GEORGETOWN. Bed & Breakfast. *American River Inn* (E-D), cnr. Orleans and Main Sts. (916) 333-4499; historic 1853 hostelry on serene grounds. Pool, spa, local wines in the evenings.

Hotels. *Georgetown Hotel* (M), Main St. (916) 333-4373; 1896 hotel with Victorian decor rooms, no private baths. Saloon on premises; with live music. *Hilltop Motel* (I-M), Hwy. 193 and South St., (916) 333-4141; TV, modern units, free coffee and ice, airport pickup.

Restaurant. *Buckeye Lodge* (M-E), 7460 Wentworth Springs Rd., (916) 333-2200; continental cuisine, steaks and seafood, cocktail bar and lounge. Reservations recommended; closed Mon.

COLOMA. Bed & Breakfast. *Vineyard House* (E), Cold Springs Rd. (916) 622-2217; 1878 hostelry in quiet setting. 7 rooms with Victorian decor; excellent restaurant serving country fare. U.S. Grant gave speech from balcony. *The Coloma Country Inn* (D), in heart of Gold Discovery State Park (916) 622-6919; historic inn, built in 1857. Country-style breakfast; hot-air ballooning and river rafting packages.

PLACERVILLE. Bed & Breakfast. *Comellack-Blair House* (E-D), 3059 Cedar Ravine Rd., (916) 622-3764; elaborate Queen Anne Victorian, circa 1895. Complimentary foothills wines and country breakfast. *Fleming Jones Homestead* (E-D), 3170 Newtown Rd., (916) 626-5840; restored 1883 farmhouse set on 11 wooded acres. Porch swing and rose garden; hot muffins, baked apples, preserves, freshly ground coffee. *James Blair House* (M-D), 2985 Clay St., (916) 626-6136; romantic 1901 Queen Anne with 3-story turret and wine cellar. Spacious gardens, fireplace, sherry in parlor. *Rupley House Inn* (E-D), (916) 626-0630; farmhouse on 50 acres, amid cows, chickens, quarterhorses, gardens and antiques. Gold panning and hiking *River Rock Inn* (E-D), 1756 Georgetown Dr., (916) 622-7640; rooms with antique furnishings and superb views of American River. Rafting at doorstep. *Chichester House* (E), 800 Spring St., (916) 626-1882; restored 1892 Victorian home, furnished with antiques. Country breakfast.

Motels. *Gold Trail Motor Lodge* (M), 1970 Broadway, (916) 622-2906; phones, TV, pool, AAA. *El Dorado Motel* (I), 1500 Broadway, (916) 622-3884; 24 rooms, TV. *Mother Lode Motel* (M), 1940 Broadway, (916) 622-0895; TV, phones, in-room coffee, pool, AAA. Also bus and truck parking. *Broadway Motel* (M), 1332 Broadway, (916) 622-3124; 43 units, phones, TV, coffee. *Hangtown Motel* (I), 1676 Broadway, (916) 622-0637; TV, free coffee.

Restaurants. *Tinker's Cove* (M-E), 263 Placerville Dr., (916) 626-8330; specialties lobster and sauteed scallops; also prime rib and steaks. Live entertainment. *Carriage Room* (I-M), 1496 Broadway, (916) 622-0471, casual lunches. Reservations. *Zoe's Restaurant & Cafe* (I-M), 301 Main St., (916) 622-9681; homemade soups and desserts are specialties, also local wines and gourmet coffee beans. Dinners 5-9 Fri.-Sun., lunch 11.30-2.30 Mon.-Sat., Sunday brunch; closed Tues. *Zachary Jacques* (E), 1821 Pleasant Valley Rd., (916) 626-8045; French cuisine, creative pastry desserts.

Dinners 5.30-10 Tues.-Sun. *Smith Flat House* (M-E), 2021 Smith Flat Rd., (916) 626-9003; well-known dining establishment housed in historic building; American fare, entertainment and dancing. Lunch Mon.-Fri., dinner daily.

AMADOR CITY. Bed & Breakfast. *Mine House Inn* (M-E), Hwy. 49, (209) 267-5900; old Keystone Mine office building with guest rooms named after original function, such as Vault, Stores, Director, Assay, Retort. 8 rooms with private baths; Victorian antiques, pool. *Culbert House Inn* (D), 10811 Water St., (209) 267-0440; 4 antique-decorated rooms in 1870s home, garden setting; full breakfast.

Restaurants. *The Cellar Restaurant* (I-M), off Main St., (209) 267-0384; lunches, fondues, salad bar. *Au Relais French Restaurant* (D), 14220 Hwy. 49, (209) 267-5636; traditional French cuisine, local and imported wines. Dinners Wed.-Sun. Reservations.

SUTTER CREEK. Bed & Breakfast. *Sutter Creek Inn* (E-D), 75 Main St., (209) 267-5606; 19 rooms with private baths, many with fireplaces and swinging beds. Hot breakfast, evening sherry. *Nine Eureka Street* (D), P.O. Box 386, Sutter Creek 95685, (209) 267-0342; lovely 1916 California bungalow with antiques, rich woods and stained glass. Rooms with baths. *The Hanford House* (E-D), 3 Hanford St., (209) 267-0747; 9 large rooms with private baths and queen beds. Continental breakfast, complimentary foothills wine. *The Foxes of Sutter Creek* (D), 77 Main St., (209) 267-5882; 3 beautiful suites with Victorian and French antiques, all with private baths. Breakfast on silver service, complimentary wine; no children, no pets.

Restaurant-Inns. *Sutter Creek Palace* (M-E), 76 Main St., (209) 267-9852; Historic inn with restaurant, patio. Lunch from 11 a.m., dinner from 5 p.m. *Bellotti Inn* (M), 53 Main St., (209) 267-5211; 1800s hostelry serving family-style Italian dinner, with fresh soups, sauces, and dressings. Also cocktail lounge, and 28 guest rooms, 15 with private baths.

Restaurants. *Harrower's Sutter Creek Cafe* (I), cnr. Amelia St. and Hwy. 49, (209) 267-5114; family lunches and dinners, specialties include homemade breads and pies; local wines. Menu changes daily. Open lunch and dinner Tues.-Sat, Sunday breakfast buffet 9-2. *The Pasty Place* (I), 35 Main St., (209) 267-0592; informal eatery specializing in King Richard Cornish pasties, soups, sandwiches, salads, quiche, croissants, cheesecake. Also tasting and sale of Shenandoah Valley wines.

JACKSON. Bed & Breakfast. *The Court Street Inn* (E-D), 215 Court St., (209) 223-0416; antique filled guest rooms with lace curtains and handmade quilts, some fireplaces. Fresh flowers, complimentary wine; spa. *Ann Marie's Country Inn* (E-D), 410 Stasal Ave., (209) 223-1452; 1892 Victorian home with porch, parlor, and 4 rooms decorated with antiques, 2 have private baths. Complimentary wine, brandy on side tables; picnic lunches, and babysitting. *Gate House Inn* (E-D), 1330 Jackson Gate Rd., (209) 223-3500; beautiful Victorian with marble fireplaces, crystal chandeliers, and antique clock collection. Well-kept gardens, pool; no children, no pets. *The Wedgewood Inn* (D), 11941 Narcissus Rd., (209) 296-4300; wooded setting; 4 antique-filled rooms with private baths. Full breakfast featuring omelettes, quiche, crepes and homemade muffins. No pets or children.

Hotels and Motels. *Country Squire Motel* (I), 1105 Jackson Gate Rd., (209) 223-1657; many rooms decorated with antiques, bridal suite boasts 1790 French furnishings. Continental breakfast; gold panning in nearby creek. Also has motel units. *Broadway Hotel* (M), 225 Broadway, (209) 223-3503; 1904 hostelry, former boarding house for miners; 15 rooms, and hot tub under gazebo. Homemade breakfast, consisting of nutbread, fruit salad, cheese, jams and coffee. *National Hotel* (I-D), 2 Water St., (209) 223-0500; historic 1862 hotel with 34 rooms, private baths, antique furnishings. Dinner in Lousiana House (downstairs) Wed.-Sun. *Jackson Holiday Lodge* (M), 850 N. Hwy. 49, (209) 223-0486; 37 units, TV, phones, coffee in lobby, pool, AAA. *Best Western Amador Inn* (M), 27 Main St., (209) 223-0211; 50 units, TV, phones, pool, restaurant, cocktail lounge. *El Campo Casa* (I-M), 12548 Kennedy Flat Rd., (at junction of Hwys. 88 & 49), (209) 223-0100; 15 rooms, TV, in-room coffee, pool, gardens, AAA.

Restaurants. *The Balcony Restaurant* (M-E), 164 Main St., (209) 223-2855; continental cuisine, with special menu Friday nights; also private dining room. Closed Sun. *Teresa's Place* (I-E), 1235 Jackson Gate Rd., (209) 223-1786; authentic Italian food, local wines, bar. Reservations; closed Wed. and Thurs. *Marlene & Glen's Dining Parlor* (M), 26 Main St., (209) 223-9951; American fare, prime rib and fish specials on Fri. and Sat.

IONE. **Bed & Breakfast.** *The Heirloom* (M-D), 214 Shakley Ln., (209) 274-4468; 1863 Colonial mansion in lovely garden setting, with verandahs, fireplaces, and a grand piano for playing; rooms decorated with antiques. French country breakfast.

VOLCANO. *St. George Hotel* (D), St. George and Main Sts., (209) 296-4458; three-story hotel, built in 1862; 19 rooms, 6 with private baths. Dinner included.

MOKELUMNE HILL. *Hotel Leger* (M-D), Main St., (209) 286-1401; historic 1860s hostelry with spacious rooms, many with private baths; complimentary coffee and rolls. Dining room and bar open daily; pool.

SAN ANDREAS. **Bed & Breakfast.** *Thorn Mansion* (D), 87 E. St. Charles St., (209) 754-1027; restored home of Sheriff Ben Thorn, who captured Black Bart. 3 acres of lush gardens with gazebo, sloping lawn with ponds, creek and waterfalls; no children, no pets. *The Robin's Nest* (E-D), 247 W. St. Charles Street, P.O. Box 1408, San Andreas 9249, (209) 754-1076; elegant Victorian country home in rural setting; rooms with private baths. Homemade breads, egg dishes and fresh fruit.

Motel. *Black Bart Inn* (M), 55 W. St. Charles Street, (209) 754-3808; 40 rooms, TV and phones, pool, coffee shop, dining room, cocktail lounge. Adjoining hotel with 25 rooms, without private baths. Also has restaurant featuring seafood buffets, live music on weekends.

ANGELS CAMP. **Bed & Breakfast.** *Cooper House* (E-D), 1184 Church St., (209) 736-2145; 3 guest rooms with private baths, full breakfast. *Utica Mansion Inn* (E-D), 1090 Utica Lane, (209) 736-4209; housed in historic building; spacious rooms with Victorian decor, private baths. Gourmet breakfast.

Motel. *Gold Country Inn* (I), 720 S. Main St., (209) 736-4611; 28 rooms, TV, phones, AAA; Perko's restaurant next door.

MURPHYS. **Bed & Breakfast.** *Dunbar House* (E-D), 271 Jones St., (209) 728-2897; beautifully restored 1880s home; 5 rooms, fresh flowers, continental breakfast.

Hotel. *Murphys Hotel* (M), 457 Main St., (209) 728-3444; refurbished 1856 hotel with 9 historic rooms named after illustrious guests, including U.S. Grant, Mark Twain and Black Bart; ask to see old guest register, where names of these and other famous guests appear. Also, adjoining motel with 20 modern units. Restaurant (M) in hotel, open daily; prime rib and fried chicken are favorites.

In **Arnold** (20 miles east): *Wehe's Meadowmont Lodge* (M), Hwy. 4

(P.O. Box E), Arnold 95223, (209) 795-1394; complete resort with restaurant, coffee shop, cocktail lounge and picnic areas; also, tennis courts, 9-hole 36-par golf course, and 75-foot heated Olympic pool. Open year-round.

COLUMBIA. Bed & Breakfast. *City Hotel* (E-D), Main St., (209) 532-1479; 1856 hostelry in historic gold rush town; 9 rooms with half baths, showers in hallway. Continental breakfast, evening sherry. Restaurant and saloon on premises. *Fallon Hotel* (M-D), 11175 Washington St., (209) 532-1470; restored 1890's hotel; 13 antique-decorated rooms.

Motel. *Columbia Inn Motel* (M), 22646 Broadway, (209) 533-0446; 24 units, TV, phone, hot tub, pool, coffee shop, restaurant and cocktail lounge.

Restaurants. *City Hotel* (E-D), Main St., (209) 532-1479; award winning restaurant with superb French cuisine; specialties include beef wellington, rack of lamb, veal piccatta, and souffle desserts. Reservations suggested. *The Columbia House* (M), cnr. State and Main Sts. (209) 532-5134; home-cooked meals; favorites are pasties, meat loaf, and home-baked rolls and buns topped with apple crisp. Seating for 165; large oak dance floor. *Arturo's* (I-M), 22758 Broadway, (209) 532-6613; fine Mexican dining.

SONORA. Bed & Breakfast. *The Ryan House* (E), 153 S. Shepherd St., (209) 533-3445; 1850s gold rush home; rooms with private baths; cherry flower garden. *Llamahall Guest Ranch* (D), 18170 Wards Ferry Rd., (209) 532-7264; 2 rooms, library and music room with fireplace. Also hot tub, sauna, and jogging trail outside. Wooded setting, with creek meandering nearby, and llamas to play with. Continental breakfast. *Serenity* (E), 15305 Bear Club Dr., (P.O. Box 3484) Sonora 95370, (209) 533-1441; period home with spacious grounds; rooms with private baths. *Barretta Gardens Inn* (E), 700 S. Barretta St., (209) 532-6039; elegant home with porch and old-fashioned gardens. Homemade breakfast. *La Casa Inglesa* (E), 18047 Lime Kiln Rd., (209) 532-5822; elegant country English home in garden setting; 4 rooms with private baths. *Lavender Hill* (M-E), 683 S. Barretta St., (209) 532-9024; restored Victorian home with 3 tastefully-decorated guest rooms; parlor, sitting room, full country breakfast. *Via Serena Ranch* (M), 18007 Via Serena Dr., (209) 532-5307; ranch house in quiet setting; 3 rooms with fireplaces, continental breakfast. *Jameson's* (M-E), 22157 Feather River Dr., (209) 532-1248; 4 rooms in country home; creekside setting, decks, game room.

Hotels and Motels. *Gunn House Motor Hotel* (M), 286 S. Washington St., (209) 532-3421; converted 1851 home, with 28 well-appointed rooms with private baths. Cocktail lounge (Josephine Room) in hotel. *Sonora Inn* (M), 160 S. Washington St., (209) 532-7468; historic 1896 hostelry, 66 rooms, phones, hot tub, exercise room, pool, restaurant and lounge. *Best Western Sonora Oaks Motor Lodge* (E-D), cnr. Hwy. 108 and Hess Ave., (209) 533-4400; 70 rooms, TV, phones, spa, pool, restaurant and lounge. *Sonora Towne House Motels* (M), 350 S. Washington St., (209) 532-3633; 112 units, TV, phones, free coffee, hot tub, pool, restaurants. *Sonora Gold Lodge* (M), 480 W. Stockton Rd., (209) 532-3952; 42 off-highway units, TV, AAA. *Miners Motel* (I-M), 18740 Hwy. 108 (cnr. Hwy. 49), (209) 532-7850. *Rail Fence Motel* (I-M), 19950 Hwy. 108 (5 miles east of Sonora), (209) 532-9191; 8 rooms, TV, in-room coffee, hot tub, pool, country setting; continental breakfast.

Restaurants. *Sonora Inn* (M), 16 S. Washington St., (209) 532-7468; open breakfast, lunch and dinner; specializing in steaks, seafood, veal. *Hemingway's* (M-E), 362 S. Stewart St., (209) 532-4900; cafe and restaurant, open lunch and dinner; closed Sun.-Mon. Creative California and Continental cuisine. *Sullivan Creek* (M-E), 1780 Mono Way, (209) 532-6767; steaks and seafood, chicken and veal, homemade pasta; family atmosphere.

SOULSBYVILLE. *Willow Springs Bed & Breakfast Inn* (M-D), 20599 Kings Court, (209) 533-2030; 1880s ranch house in country setting, with 4 rooms and a cottage; full breakfast.

TUOLUMNE. *Oak Hill Ranch* (E-D), 18550 Conally Ln., (209) 928-4717; country Victorian rooms; gourmet breakfast.

TWAIN HARTE. *Twain Harte's Bed & Breakfast* (M-D), 18864 Manzanita Dr., (209) 586-3311; wooded setting, large decks, sunroom, antique furnishings. *Wildwood Inn* (M), 22960 Meadow Ln., (209) 586-2900; 30 rooms, TV, phones, AAA. *Twain Harte's Inn* (M), Twain Harte Dr., (209) 586-7201; 70 units, TV, phones, restaurant and lounge.

JAMESTOWN. Bed & Breakfast. *The Palm Hotel* (E-D), 10382 Willow St., (209) 984-3429; elegant, period hostelry with 9 well-appointed rooms.
   Hotels and Motels. *National Hotel* (M), Main St., (209) 984-3446; one of California's oldest hostelries, operating since 1859; Gold Rush decor in guest rooms. Restaurant and bar on premises. *Royal Hotel* (M), Main St., (209) 984-5271; beautiful turn-of-the-century hotel with comfortable rooms. *Railtown Motel* (M), 10301 Willow St., (209) 984-3332; modern units, TV, phones, pool, spa.
   Restaurants. *The Smoke Cafe* (I-M), Main St., (209) 984-3733; fine Mexican food. Closed Mon. *National Hotel & Restaurant* (M), Main St., (209) 984-3446; superb Italian-American cuisine. *Jamestown Hotel & Restaurant* (M-E), Main St., (209) 984-3902; house specialty: prime rib; also home-made pasta and seafood. Courtyard for outdoor dining in summer. Open daily.

COULTERVILLE. *Yosemite Americana Inn* (I), 10407 Hwy. 49, (209) 878-3407; modern motel units, TV, in-room coffee, gift shop. Also full hookup RV parking.

MARIPOSA. Bed & Breakfast. *Meadow Creek Ranch* (E-D), 2669 Triangle Rd., (209) 966-3843; 1857 stage stop; 3 rooms upstairs, with baths downstairs. Country breakfast, freshly ground coffee. *Granny's Garden* (M-E), 7333 Hwy. 49 North (209) 377-8342; 1896 farmhouse; 2 rooms, share bath. Continental breakfast; antique shop on premises. Closed Oct.-May.
   Motels. *Mariposa Lodge* (M), Hwy. 49 (209) 966-3607; 37 spacious rooms, TV, in-room coffee, phones, pool and spa, AAA. *Miner's Inn* (M), cnr. Hwys. 49 & 140, (209) 742-7777; 40 units, TV, phones. *Yosemite Way Station* (M-E), 4999 Hwy. 140, (209) 966-7545; 78 rooms, TV, phones, spa, pool.
   Restaurants. *Charles Street Dinner House* (M), cnr. Hwy. 140 & 7th, (209) 966-2366; steaks and seafood, homemade soup, 25 entrees, 12 homemade desserts. Reservations recommended. *Tink's Little Acre* (M), cnr. Hwy. 140 & 12th (209) 966-5707; old fashioned cooking, open breakfast, lunch, dinner; featured in People magazine. Some baked specialties. *China Station* (M), cnr. Hwys. 140 & 49, (209) 966-3889; Mandarin and Cantonese specialties. *Maria's Cantina* (I-M), 4995 5th, (209) 966-5544; great Mexican food; favorites are chili relleno, spicy chili verde and carne asada, served with homemade lemon sherbet. Closed Sun.

OAKHURST. Motels. *Yosemite Gateway Best Western Inn* (M-E), 40530 Hwy. 41, (209) 683-2378; modern motel units, TV, phones, pool, family units, *Rustic Pines Lodge* (I), 40489 Hwy. 41, (209) 683-7664; 20 units, TV, pool. *Sierra Sky Ranch* (M), 50552 Road 632, (209) 683-4433;

28 units, pool, restaurant, golf course.

In **Fish Camp** (10 miles northwest): *Narrow Gauge Inn* (E-D), Hwy. 41, (209) 683-7720; 27 units, TV, restaurant. Tours on scenic railway available.

At **Coarsegold**. *The Coarsegold Inn-Restaurant* (M), Hwy. 41, Coarsegold; (209) 683-4620. Specialties: steaks, seafood, homemade pies. Live music on weekends. Closed Tues.

 TOURIST INFORMATION. Visitor information is readily available throughout the Gold Country. Especially useful are the Chambers of Commerce which have local maps, calendars of events, listings for lodging, dining and recreational facilities, special tourist publications and literally a wealth of information. Museums and state park offices are also excellent value, as they are generally open on weekends; you can usually find local literature, maps and other bits of information at these, and some even carry books of local interest. Bookstores are yet another valuable source of information, with an extensive range of books on local history and regional interest; some of the other area merchants also carry selective titles in the regional category.

If you intend to travel widely in the region, a complete Gold Country map is much to be recommended; the Golden Chain Council publishes the *Mother Lode Highway Map*, and Compass Maps' *Gold Map* is also quite good. In addition, most of the Gold Country counties publish their own, detailed maps.

Chambers of Commerce and Information Bureaus. *Amador County Chamber of Commerce*, cnr. Hwys. 49 & 88 (P.O. Box 596), Jackson 95642; (209) 223-0350. Walking tour maps of all major county towns, tour map of wine country, and free tourist publications. Hours: 9-5 Mon.-Fri., sometimes also open weekends. After hours, tourist information can be found on the rack outside the chamber office.

Calaveras County Chamber of Commerce, 753 S. Main St., (P.O. Box 111), Angels Camp 95222, (209) 736-4444. Walking tour map of Angels Camp downtown, and map of town's mine sites. 9-5 weekdays. If chamber office is closed, ask at museum next door for maps and brochures.

Eastern Madera County Chamber of Commerce, Civic Circle (P.O. Box 369), Oakhurst 93644; (209) 683-7766. Open Mon.-Fri. 10-4, Sat. 1-4. *Tourist Information Center* next door, with brochures, maps and other visitor information; open 7 days. Also, *Bass Lake Chamber of Commerce*, P.O. Box 126, Bass Lake 93604; (209) 642-3676.

El Dorado County Chamber of Commerce, 542 Main St., Placerville 95667; (916) 626-2344. Maps, brochures, calendar of events; also tour maps of Apple Hill orchards and Christmas Tree farms. Open Mon.-Fri. 9.30-4.00.

Mariposa County Chamber of Commerce, cnr. Jones St. and Hwy. 49 (P.O. Box 425), Mariposa 95338; (209) 966-2456. Local tourist publications, maps, brochures, lodging directory. Open 8-4.30 daily.

Tuolumne County Chamber of Commerce, 19445 W. Stockton Rd. (P.O. Box 277), Sonora 95370; (209) 532-4212. Open Mon.-Fri. 10-4). Also *Tuolumne County Visitors Bureau*, 16 W. Stockton Rd. (P.O. Box 4020), Sonora 95370; (209) 533-4420. Information on lodging, camping, restaurants, events of interest, and recreational activities. Open Mon.-Fri. 10-4. Another information bureau is located at the Yosemite Junction (cnr. Hwys. 108 & 120), on the road to Oakdale; open weekdays, (209) 984-INFO.

LOCAL TRANSPORTATION. In **Placerville**. *El Dorado Transit* services the Placerville area on a regular basis. For timetable information call (916) 626-2143.

In **Jackson Area**. *Amador Rapid Transit*, Jackson. Daily schedule includes 6 shuttles between Jackson and Sutter Creek, 4 runs to Ione, 3 runs to Plymouth, 9 runs up-country; also on-call service is available for Volcano and Pine Grove. Fare is 75¢ single, or $20.00 for an unlimited monthly pass. For more information call (209) 223-BUSS.

In the **Angels Camp-Murphys Area**. *Calaveras Transit Co.*, Murphys. The bus company services the county on a regular basis. For information and timetable, call (209) 728-1193.

In the **Sonora Area**. *Sonora Community Transit Services* has a scheduled bus service in the Sonora area; fare is 60¢ within Sonora, and 70¢ outside Sonora. For a timetable and more information, call (209) 533-0404.

SEASONAL EVENTS. There are hundreds of small and big events held throughout the Gold Country every year. Most of the county fairs and other big events are usually held as scheduled, though dates for some of the smaller events are subject to change, depending on weather and availability of funds. We therefore recommend that you check with the respective chambers of commerce for exact dates for events.

(Abbreviations: AC-Amador County; CC-Calaveras County; EM-Eastern Madera County; BL-Bass Lake; EC-El Dorado County; MC-Mariposa County; TC-Tuolumne County.)

JANUARY. *Dodge Ridge Ski Events*, Pinecrest (TC); assorted ski events, including NASTAR races. *Serbian Christmas & New Year*, Jackson (AC); celebrations held during first weekend of month.

FEBRUARY. *Dodge Ridge Ski Events*, Pinecrest (TC); assorted ski events throughout the month.

MARCH. *Dandelion Days Flea Market and Celebration*, Jackson (AC); 250 booths, swing and sway rhythm band, staged gunfighter duels, tug of war; held on St. Patrick's Day weekend. *Daffodil Hill*, near Volcano (AC); historic 4-acre ranch opened to public during the middle of the month; 500,000 daffodils and other flowers, walks, picnicking, photography. *Snowshoe Thompson Day*, Placerville (EC); festivities on third weekend of month. *Dodge Ridge Ski Events*, Pinecrest (TC); assorted events for ski enthusiasts.

APRIL. Second Weekend. *AAUW Historical Home & Building Tour*, Sutter Creek (AC); see *Tours* section. *Daffodil Hill*, near Volcano (AC); historic ranch with 500,000 daffodils and other flowers in bloom, walks, picnicking and photography until approximately the middle of the month.

Fourth Weekend. *Mountain Men Rendezvous*, Railroad Flat (CC); display of marksmanship with Flintlock rifles. *Mother Lode Dixieland Jazz Festival*, Jackson and Sutter Creek (AC); jam sessions at "watering holes" in area, with eight to ten jazz bands featured.

MAY. First Weekend. *Ione Homecoming*. Ione (AC); arts and crafts shows, dances, parade, Miss Ione beauty pageant. *Snyders Annual Valley Springs Rock Pow-Wow*, Valley Springs (CC); rock hound celebration with rocks and minerals, arts and crafts shows, entertainment, demonstrations, barbeque, and weekend camping. *Firemen's Muster*, Columbia (TC); fire brigades compete in various fire drills using antique fire engines and fire-fighting equipment; parade at the end of the day. *Bass Lake Fishing Derby*, Bass Lake (BL); cash prizes for tagged trout worth $20,000, and 99 other trout worth $3,000.

Second Weekend. *Coarsegold Rodeo*, Coarsegold (EM); one of the most colorful rodeos in the southern mine region.

Third Weekend. *Calaveras County Fair & Jumping Frog Jubilee*, Angels Camp (CC); an original American celebration featuring world-renowned frog jumping contest with prize money for winner; "frog rentals" available at fairgrounds. Other festivities include stage shows such as Bellamy Brothers, and rodeos, destruction derbies and carnival rides. *Hangtown Rodeo*, Placerville (EC).

Fourth Weekend. *Fiddletown at the Fair Days*, Plymouth (AC); regional fiddling contests, concerts, arts and crafts shows.

JUNE. First Weekend. *Bass Lake Car Show*, Bass Lake (BL); display of custom and classic cars and trucks from throughout the state. *Columbia Diggins*, Columbia (TC); recreation of gold rush days with tent city, and food and events of late 1800s gold mining era.

Second Weekend. *Butterfly Days*, Mariposa (MC); overnight wagon ride from Wawone to Mariposa, midget auto races, dancing, barbeque, arts and crafts show, parade. *Italian Picnic and Parade*, Sutter Creek (AC); century-old event featuring carnival rides, food and drink stalls, barbeque, and parade. *Fiddlers Jamboree*, Railroad Flat (CC); music, arts and crafts, mud wrestling, husband calling contest, greased pig contest, bingo. *Dixieland Jazz Festival*, Jamestown (TC); half-dozen or so jazz bands play favorites at local "watering holes." *Country Summer Games*, Bass Lake (BL); "anything that floats" contest, California Gold Panning Championships, bikini contest, horseshoe pitching tournament, food and entertainment.

Third Weekend. *Days of Kit Carson*, Jackson (AC); overnight wagon ride from Buckhorn to Jackson, Western Dress contest, mule wagon rides, pancake breakfast, Kit Carson dance, art exhibits, *Columbia Fly-In*, Columbia (TC); 15-year-old event featuring hundreds of vintage airplanes at aircraft display at Columbia Airport, dinner and dance, Sunday Hanger Breakfast. *Old West Days*, Groveland (TC); parade, dancing, and western fanfare, including mock hanging.

Fourth Weekend. *Highway 50 Wagon Train*, Placerville (EC); 30 covered wagons arrive at Placerville from Carson City, Nevada, journeying several days; street dancing and other festivities commemorating historic event. *Annual Quilt Faire*, Arnold (CC); display of over 100 exquisite quilts.

JULY. First Weekend. *Annual Boat Parade & Fireworks Display*. Bass Lake (BL); decorated boat parade, and fireworks display over lake. *Annual Pony Express Days Parade*, Pollock Pines (EC); pony express recreation, parade and dancing.

Third Weekend. *Mother Lode Fair*, Sonora (TC); carnival rides, stage entertainment and ground acts, country western music, horse show, livestock exhibitions and awards, pony express races, horseback tug of war, destruction derby and four-wheel-drive pull.

Fourth Weekend. *El Dorado County Fair*, Placerville (EC); rides, entertainment, gold exhibit, wine tasting with focus on local wines, vintage car displays, four-wheel-drive pulls, dancing, pageants, and wheel-barrow races commemorating one-time town resident John Studebaker who made wheel-barrows for miners here.

AUGUST. First Weekend. *Amador County Fair*, Plymouth (AC); headliner stage entertainment, logging shows, rodeos, horse show, extensive livestock exhibition, antique engines display, destruction derby. *Sierra Pines Marathon Relay*, Bass Lake (BL); marathon features four-person relay teams, twice around the lake.

Second Weekend. *Annual Arts & Crafts Festival*, Bass Lake (BL); arts and crafts show with over 100 booths, entertainment, food and drink stalls.

Third Weekend. *Bass Lake Half-Marathon*, Bass Lake (BL); once-around-the-lake marathon.

Fourth Weekend. *Annual Mother Lode Show*, Placerville (EC); over 40 antique dealers display and sell their ware.

SEPTEMBER. First Weekend. *Annual Mariposa County Fair and Homecoming*, Mariposa (MC); one of the best small county fairs in the state, featuring saddle roping contest, rodeos, destruction derbies, entertainment, dancing, carnival rides, and a variety of exhibits. *Sourdough Days*, Sutter Creek (AC); arts and crafts fair, home-baked goodies and preserves, historic home tours. *Ebbetts Pass Arts & Crafts in Action*, Arnold (CC); arts and crafts fair, with food and drink stalls. *Strawberry Bluegrass Festival*, Groveland (TC); "strawberry jammin'" in enchanting Yosemite setting; some camping. *Annual Chicken Fly-Off and Air Show*, Georgetown (EC); all-star show, chicken races, pig roast, entertainment.

Second Weekend. *Mi-Wuk Indian Acorn Festival*, Tuolumne (TC); traditional Native American handicrafts, tribal dances, song, hand games, and pit barbequed beef dinner with special acorn bread. *Black Bart Days*, San Andreas (CC); arts and crafts show, food and drink stalls, music, dancing, parade. *Airport Day*, San Andreas (CC); airshow with experimental aircraft, model airplanes and displays, parachute artists.

Fourth Weekend. *Indian Big Time Days*, Chaw'Se Indian Grinding Rock State Historic Park, near Volcano (AC); celebration by Miwok Indians, with ceremonial dances, games, food stalls, handicraft booths, movies and slide shows.

OCTOBER. First Weekend. *Antique Show and Sale*, Sonora (TC); over 30 antique dealers represented. *Lumberjack Day*, West Point (CC); axe throwing contest, stock sawing, hand bucking, music, barbeque dinner, parade. *Murphys Oktoberfest*, Murphys (CC); arts and crafts show, food stalls, entertainment.

NOVEMBER. Fourth Weekend. *Annual Christmas Faire*, Sonora (TC); extensive range of crafts, Christmas items and decorations, continuous stage entertainment.

DECEMBER. *Amador County Christmas Activities*, in Amador City, Sutter Creek, Volcano and Jackson, during first and second weekends of the month; activities ranging from an open holiday house in Sutter Creek, to the Festival of Lights in Volcano. Check with Amador County Chamber of Commerce for events and dates.

STAGECOACH TOURS. *Columbia Stage Lines*; headquartered at the Wells Fargo Express building in the Columbia State Historic Park. Journey through Columbia's back country on board an authentic Abbot & Downing Concord Stagecoach built in 1874; 15-minute rides along a loop trail will take you through some picturesque terrain, and you can even ride shotgun — up next to the stagecoach driver. Stage fares are $3.00 adults, $2.50 children; riding shotgun: $4.00 adults, $3.50 children. For information call (209) 785-2244 or (209) 785-2263, or write Columbia Stage Line, P.O. Box 268, Angels Camp 95222.

Yosemite Stagecoach Lines; located at the Ol-Nip lodge at Nipinnawasee (7 miles north of Oakhurst on Highway 49). Old-fashioned tours to Yosemite and the Miami Creek waterfalls, leading over original, historic roads. Trail time is around 2 hours, and the tours include a ranch breakfast, lunch on the trail, and barbeque steak dinner; also some gold panning. Tour cost: $62.50 adults, $31.25 children. Tours are by reservation only; for more information and reservations, call (209) 683-2668.

WALKING TOURS. The Amador County Chamber of Commerce publishes "walking tour" maps for most major county towns, including *Jackson, Ione, Amador City, Sutter Creek, Volcano, Pine Grove, Plymouth* and *Drytown*; Volcano and Sutter Creek are especially delightful.

In Calaveras County, the two most notable towns given to exploring on foot are *Angels Camp* and *Murphys*. Maps detailing Angels Camp's historic downtown buildings are available at most local merchants, particularly motels, for around 25¢; and a layout of the in-town mine sites can be obtained from the local museum on Main Street. A walking tour map of Murphys can be obtained at the Old Timer's Museum on Main Street. Other county towns of interest are *Mokelumne Hill* and *San Andreas*, each with a small Main Street dotted with a handful of gold rush era buildings — quite rewarding to walkers.

Farther south, in Tuolumne County, the beautifully restored gold rush town of *Columbia* is a walker's paradise, with its lovely tree-shaded streets lined with frame cottages and iron-shuttered brick buildings; an excellent town map, pinpointing all the historic buildings, can be found in the "Columbia Gazette Visitors' Guide," available at most local stores. Also *Sonora* and *Jamestown* have interesting main streets, ideally suited to walking, with several century-old buildings to be explored along these. A map of Sonora, with illustrations of the town's historic buildings, is available for a nominal charge from the Visitors Bureau on W. Stockton St. or Charley's Bookstore on N. Washington St.

In Mariposa County, a map of *Mariposa* pinpointing places of historical interest is available at the local museum or Chamber of Commerce; the downtown area has buildings of historic interest, and is given to being explored on foot. *Coulterville*, 28 miles north of Mariposa on Hwy. 49, has a main street where all the buildings date from the 1800s or early 1900s. It is an excellent place to explore on foot, with a public park quite close to the main street. A walking tour map of the town is published by the Yosemite Americana Inn of Coulterville.

HISTORIC HOME TOURS. *AAUW Historical Home & Building Tour*, Sutter Creek. Self-guided tours of selected historic homes and buildings, including some bed and breakfast inns, are offered every spring, usually in the month of April; tour cost: $8.00. For information and reservations, call (209) 267-0024, or write 25 Foothill Dr., Sutter Creek 95685.

MINE TOURS. Hidden Treasure Gold Mine, Main St. (P.O. Box 28), Columbia 95310; (209) 532-9693 or 533-4819. Guided tours of a 700-foot mine tunnel in an operating gold mine, originally discovered in 1879. Tour guide will show you what a quartz vein looks like, and explain the phenomenon of stopes, side-drifts and glory holes. Courtesy bus leaves for the mine from the Columbia Mine Supply Store on Main Street. Store opens at 9 a.m., and tours begin at 10.30, daily May-Sept. and on weekends the rest of the year; minimum 4 persons on tour, $5.00 per person. Group rates and special tours are available. Also, gold panning lessons are given at the supply store.

Kennedy Mine, Jackson. Guided tours of the surface works of the historic Kennedy Mine, which include the cement office building and change house, and close-up views of the 150-foot headframe and the ruins of the stamp mill. Tours are conducted by former miners and knowledgeable guides during Labor Day weekend, 10-4; tour cost is around $4.00 per person. For more information contact the Hospice of Amador, 13488 Roan Ct., Sutter Creek 95685; (209) 223-3390.

Gold Bug Mine, at the Bedford City Park on Bedford Ave., Placerville. Self-guided tours of a hard-rock gold mine; two tunnels, 362 feet and 147 feet long, respectively, both illuminated, are open to the public. On a hill above the mine one can explore the remains of a stamp mill. The park also has some good picnicking possibilities. Open 9-5.

Amador's Mining Tour. Self-guided driving-walking tour of Amador County mines — the *Kennedy, Argonaut, Central Eureka, Keystone,* and *Plymouth Consolidated.*

The famous *Kennedy Tailing Wheels* can be visited in the Kennedy Wheels Park on Jackson Gate Road, just outside Jackson, across from where the *Kennedy Mine* headframe can also be seen in the distance; the mine produced over $34 million in gold between 1900 and 1942, and reached a depth of 5,912 feet before closing — the deepest mine in North America at the time.

The *Argonaut Mine* headframe is located on a hill just west of Jackson, reached by way of Argonaut Lane, off Hwy. 49. The mine began operating in the 1860s and produced over $25 million in gold, reaching a depth of 5,570 feet, vertically. In 1922, Argonaut was the scene of one of the worst mining tragedies in the history of the state, when 47 miners became trapped and eventually died from gasses released by a mine fire.

The *Central Eureka Mine* headframe can be seen on a hill above Sutter Hill (just south of Sutter Creek), east off Hwy. 49 on Ridge Road (or State Rt. 104). The Central Eureka was one of the richest mines in the region, with an estimated gold output of $36 million. The mine was originally developed by Alvinza Hayward, California's first mining millionaire; it closed in 1958.

The *Keystone Mine* is located at the southern end of Amador City, its headframe overhanging a hill on the east side of the highway (49). The mine produced roughly $24 million in gold and reached a depth of 2,680 feet; it operated from 1853 to 1942. The Keystone office building, across from the headframe on the west side of the highway, is now a delightful bed and breakfast inn, the Mine House.

Farther north in Plymouth, some tailing piles can be seen on the east side of the highway, at the site of the *Plymouth Consolidated Mines.* Plymouth Consolidated operated from 1883 to 1947, reached a depth of 4,550 feet, and produced over $13.5 million in gold.

Other headframes, ruins and tailing piles can be seen on the back road between Amador City and Drytown; these include remains of the *Bunker Hill Mine,* the *Fremont Mine* and the *Little Amador Mine.*

GOLD PROSPECTING TOURS. Most popular for panning gold is of course the South Fork of the American River, just above Coloma where the original gold discovery was made. Several resorts and inns in the area, particularly those situated on creeks and rivers, also offer panning. In fact, most rivers and streams in the Mother Lode are good places to pan for gold, but for first-time prospectors it is advisable to join an organized gold tour, where one can learn to pan, use a sluice box, "read" a stream, snipe (locate gold in crevices), and, on some of the tours, instruction is also given in the use of a dredge — the tool of modern day miners.

Gold Prospecting Expeditions of 18172 Main St., Jamestown, conduct daily gold prospecting tours: 1-3 hours, full day, 3-4 days, or weekend tours; prices range from $5.00 for panning just outside the old livery stable on Main Street, to $575.00 for a weekend helicopter trip into remote river canyons where dredging equipment is also available. Tours are guided, and instruction is given in panning, sluicing, sniping, dredging, metal detecting, and pocket hunting (locating gold bearing veins). Most propecting equipment is supplied. For more information call (209) 984-4162, or write Gold Prospecting Expeditions, P.O. Box 974, Jamestown 95327.

Roaring Camp Mining Co., off Hwy. 88 at Pine Grove, offers 4-hour tours of its operating gold mine in the Mokelumne River Canyon, and its Wildlife and Mining Museum; and instruction is given in gold panning, sluicing, sniping and dredging. Also, rustic prospectors' cabins are available for rent at the camp — $280.00 for 2 persons for a week. In spring, a gold prospecting seminar is held here for those wishing to learn more about prospecting. For information and cabin reservations, call (209) 296-4100, or write Roaring Camp Mining Co., P.O. Box 278, Pine Grove 95665. Roaring Camp also has an information office at the corner of Hwys. 88 and 49 in Jackson.

Gold Country Prospecting, 3119 Turner St., Placerville, offers gold prospecting tours to the American River, 5 miles upstream from the site of the gold discovery. Instruction is given in panning, sniping and sluicing, and a visit to a real hardrock gold mine is included, where one can learn about gold veins. Tours are by reservation, daily; tour cost is $35.00 adults, $15.00 children. For reservations and information call (916) 622-2484.

HISTORIC RAILROAD TOURS. Sierra Railway, Railtown 1897, 5th Ave., Jamestown 95327; (209) 984-3953. Railroad dates from 1897, originally built to service the mining and lumbering communities of the county. It has a 26-acre *Roundhouse* complex with an original turntable and century-old maintenance shops with belt-driven machinery, all still in use and open to tours; also on display are three steam-powered locomotives — a 4-6-0 Rogers (No. 3) built in 1891, a 2-8-0 Baldwin (No. 28) built in 1922, and a 2-8-0 Mikado (No. 34) built in 1925; No. 3 is the Hollywood favorite, having starred in at least a dozen feature and TV films, including such all-time favorites as "Petticoat Junction," "High Noon" and "The Gambler." *Roundhouse Tours* are conducted daily in summer, 10-4; tour cost: $1.75 adults, $1.00 children. *Rail excursions* are offered on weekends in summer, June-Sept.; for a timetable and more information, contact the park.

Yosemite Mountain & Sugar Pine R.R. Hwy. 41 (2 miles south of Fish Camp or 11 miles north of Oakhurst), Fish Camp 93623; (209) 683-

7273. Early 1900s logging railroad, with two types of locomotives: "Model A" Jenny, and the steam-powered Shay. Excursions will take you through beautiful Lewis Creek Canyon, passing by such scenic points as Horseshoe Curve, Honey Hill Junction, and Springs Crossing. Seating is on carved logs placed on flat cars, and a picnic area is available enroute where passengers can disembark and snack. A *Moonlight Special* is offered on weekends, June-Sept.; this includes chuckwagon buffet dinner, beverages and western entertainment. There is also a museum, a sandwich shop and gift shop at the depot, and the adjoining Narrow Gauge Inn offers excellent accommodations. Tour cost: *Steam Train* $7.00 adults, $3.75 children; *Model A Jenny* $5.00 adults, $2.75 children; *Moonlight Special* $20.00 adults, $10.50 children. Reservations are recommended for all excursions.

 CAVE TOURS. Moaning Cavern, 5330 Moaning Cave Rd., Vallecito; take Parrots Ferry Rd. north from Columbia about 8 miles, or, from Vallecito about a mile south (Moaning Cave Rd. goes off Parrots Ferry Rd.). This is California's largest public cavern, large enough to hold the Statue of Liberty and still have room to spare. Guided tours lead down a 100-foot spiral staircase into the spectacular main chamber which is filled with gigantic crystalline formations. 13,000-year-old remains of prehistoric people can be seen in the cave, and tour guide narrates 300 million years of geological history and tells about explorations that have traced the cavern down some 410 feet. An alternative entry into the main chamber is by rappeling 180 feet. Rappeling equipment, hard hat, coveralls and gloves are provided. The caves are open daily 9-6 in summer and 10-4 in winter. Cost of 45-minute *Traditional Tour* is $4.50 adults, $2.25 children; the *Rappel* is $11.00 in addition to tour cost; and the 3-hour *Adventure Tour* is $32.00. For more information call (209) 736-2708, or write Moaning Cavern, P.O. Box 78, Vallecito 95251.

Mercer Caverns; located about a mile outside Murphys on Sheep Ranch Rd. Lighted passageways lead through 8 assorted chambers filled with fascinating crystalline formations of stalagmites, stalactites, helictites, flowstones, curtains and columns, in a variety of textures, shapes and sizes; there are such curiosities as Angels Wings, Organ Loft, Chinese Meat Market, and Solomon's Thumb; there is also an especially noteworthy column and a large corral-type formation. 232 steps lead into the caverns, and 208 steps out again. Caverns are open daily 9-5 in summer, and 11-4 on weekends and holidays in winter. Cost of 40-minute guided tour is $4.50 adults, $2.25 children. For more information call (209) 728-2101, or write Mercer Caverns, P.O. Box 509, Murphys 95247.

California Caverns-Cave City, 9565 Cave City Rd. (off Mountain Ranch Rd., 9 miles east of San Andreas), Mountain Ranch. Guided tours are conducted through a series of well-illuminated passageways and chambers which were once visited by renowned naturalist John Muir, and writers Mark Twain and Bret Harte. View dazzling formations and down-growing crystals seen hanging from archways, most of them described in Muir's "Mountains of California." Also explore deep, clear lakes within the caverns, and several deeper passageways where one must crawl through tightspots and climb slopes with ropes and ladders; hard hats, coveralls and gloves are provided for these "Wild Cave Tours." Cost for the 5-hour *Wild Cave Tour* (by reservation only) is $49.00; and the 80-minute *Walking Tour* is $4.00 adults, $2.00 children. Caverns are open daily 10-5 July through Oct., and on weekends in Nov. *Wild Cave Tours* leave at 9 a.m. For information and reservations call (209) 736-2708, or write California Caverns, P.O. Box 78, Vallecito 95251.

SPECIAL ATTRACTION. *Daffodil Hill.* A 4-acre hillside ranch, located 3 miles above Volcano off Ram's Horn Grade, or 13 miles east of Sutter Creek on the Sutter Creek-Volcano Road. For about six weeks each spring, usually from mid-March until the end of April, the hillside is covered with over 500,000 daffodils and other flowers. There are at least 300 varieties of daffodils, most common being the large yellow King Alfreds and the lovely white Mountain Hoods, and several hyacinths, crocus, tulips, violets and lilacs are scattered around in an assortment of antique pottery. Narrow foot-trails meander through the gardens for closer viewing, and there is a picnic area by the front gates of the ranch. Daffodil Hill is opened to the public when 25% or more of the flowers are in bloom, and closed for the season when only 25% or so remain. There is no admission fee, but donations are accepted for a bulb fund. For more information contact the Amador County Chamber of Commerce (209) 223-0350, or Mc-Laughlin's Daffodil Hill (209) 296-7048.

 MUSEUMS. *Gold Discovery Museum;* located in the Marshall Gold Discovery State Historic Park at Coloma, on Back St. Interpretive center with nature displays, and recount of gold discovery story illustrated with histories of James W. Marshall, the discoverer, and John Sutter; also ore samples and gold rush mining tools. Outdoor displays of stamp mills, hydraulic monitors, arrastra and sluice box. Half-hour Encyclopedia Brittanica film on early years of gold rush; Gold Country books and postcards for sale. Open 10-5 daily; admission: $3.00. (916) 622-3470.

Placerville Historical Museum, 524 Main St., Placerville. Housed in 1852 stone-brick building. Gold rush era picks, pans, shovels and sluice box; miniature model of stamp mill, a turn-of-the century washing machine, some pioneer clothing and household items, and a few antique typewriters. Open Sat.-Sun., 12-4. (916) 626-0773.

El Dorado County Historical Society Museum, 100 Placerville Dr. (at the county fairgrounds), Placerville. Artifacts of local historical interest, representing all eras of county history. Hours: 10-4 Wed.-Sun. (916) 626-2250.

Fiddletown Chinese Museum, cnr. Oleta Rd. and Jibboom St., Fiddletown. Housed in 1850s adobe hut, once the home of a Chinese herb doctor; 19th century artifacts, mostly items from herb doctor's trade. Open 12-4 on weekends, May-Sept.

Amador County Museum, Church St., Jackson. Housed in old Brown House (1858), the oldest residential building in Jackson. Beautifully restored rooms, including kitchen, with several original furniture pieces and decorative items, depicting life in the 1800s. Tour of working scale model of stamp mill, which actually pulverizes small rocks into sand, and Kennedy Tailing Wheel. Outdoor displays of mining equipment, and restored model of a 56-foot narrow-gauge locomotive which starred as the "Hooterville Cannonball" in the TV series *Petticoat Junction.* Museum hours: 10-4 Wed.-Sun. No admission fee; donations accepted. Tour: $1.00 adults, 50¢ children (209) 223-6386.

Chaw'Se Cultural Center; located in the Indian Grinding Rock State Historic Park on Pine Grove-Volcano Road, 1½ miles from either Volcano or Pine Grove. Display of Indian artifacts, including baskets, weavings, jewelry and tools; slide show of cultural interest. Open weekends 9.30-4. Park fee is $3.00, which allows entry to the cultural center. (209) 296-7488.

Calaveras County Historical Museum, 30 N. Main St., San Andreas. Housed in original Calaveras County Courthouse. Displays of 19th century life, exhibits of early mining, Miwok Indian artifacts, and "Black Bart" exhibit in adjoining jailhouse. The complex also houses the old County Archives, consisting of probate records, mining and land claims, and deeds of sorts. Open daily 11-4 in summer. (209) 754-4203.

City of Angels Museum, 753 S. Main St., Angels Camp. Excellent display of mining memorabilia and locomotives which served Angels Camp. Working model of stamp mill, early Frog Jubilee souvenirs, pioneer clothing and household items, collections of antique guns and knives, ore samples, antique gramophones and organs, and a variety of miners' tools. Open daily 10-4 in summer and weekends rest of the year; admission: 50¢. (209) 736-2963.

Old Timer Museum, cnr. Main St. and San Domingo Rd., Murphys. Housed in historic Traver Building, dating from 1856. Splendid collection of gold rush memorabilia, including two or three antique gun collections; ore samples, old photographs and "wanted" posters, and pioneer artifacts. Books and maps of local interest for sale. Open Thurs.-Sun., 12-4, June-Sept.; weekends 12-4 rest of the year. Admission: 50¢ adults, 25¢ children. No phone.

Tuolumne County Museum, 188 W. Bradford Ave., Sonora. Museum housed in old county jail. Displays centered around history of Tuolumne County; antiques, artifacts, old photographs, Mark Twain exhibit. Some local literature available. Open 10-4 Mon.-Sat. (209) 532-1317.

Wm. Cavalier Museum, cnr. Main and State Sts., Columbia. Housed in old Knapp building, dating from 1854. Relics of gold rush era; items include 1800s furniture pieces, old lithographs and photographs, an antique 16 x 20 glass plate camera, ore samples from area, and Indian artifacts. Open during park hours, 10-5 daily.

Columbia Gazette & Printing Museum, Washington St., Columbia. Housed in historic 1850s newspaper building, with ancient bookshop. Antique presses and other printing equipment; recount of history of journalism in California. Open during park hours, 10-5.

Knights Ferry Historical Center, Main St., Knights Ferry. Housed in old mill building, built from stone-brick. Interpretive center with exhibits of ore samples, and recount of town history and building of the mill. No admission fee. Open weekends 10-5. (209) 881-3318.

Northern Mariposa County History Center, cnr. Hwys. 49 & 132, Coulterville. Old mining photographs, pioneer clothing, and items of local historical interest. Museum housed in ruins of old Coulter Hotel. Open 10-4 Mon.-Sat. in summer, and weekends in winter. (209) 878-3015.

Mariposa County Museum, cnr. 12th & Jessie (just off Hwy. 140), Mariposa. Replicas of gold rush days; display of mining equipment, printing equipment, school rooms and old time apothecary; larger pieces of mining equipment, including restored 5-stamp mill, on museum grounds. Gold Country books and postcards for sale. Open daily 10-4 in summer, weekends rest of the year; closed January. (209) 966-2924.

Nathan Sweet Memorial Museum; located in Fresno Flats Historical Park on Road 427, Oakhurst. Museum housed in old schoolhouse, dating from 1874; items of historical interest donated by local residents, including pioneer clothing, schoolhouse displays, antique cameras, and early 1800s handloom. Park and museum open 1-3 Tues.-Sat., 1-4 Sun.; museum tours: $1.00 adults, 50¢ children. (209) 683-6570.

FOOTHILLS WINERIES. There are presently some 27 wineries in the region, most of them small, family owned and operated, and housed in restored barns or century-old stone cellars. Tasting tours of these are especially delightful, with the winemakers and winery owners usually there to show you around. Several of the estates have tree-shaded, scenic picnic areas on the premises, and it is worthwhile to take along a picnic lunch to enjoy with the local wines.

Following is a list of the region's wineries and the types of wines they offer. (For detailed information on the wineries, write Sierra Foothills Winery Association, P.O. Box 425, Somerset, CA 95684.)

Amador Foothill Winery, 12500 Steiner Rd., Plymouth 95669. Energy efficient winery producing primarily Zinfandel, White Zinfandel and Sauvignon Blanc. Picnic area on premises. Open weekends 12-5. (209) 245-6307.

Argonaut Winery, 13675 Mt. Echo Drive, Ione 95640. Annually produces 2,000-3,000 cases of Zinfandel, Barbera, Sauvignon Blanc, and Syrah. Call for tasting hours. (209) 274-4106.

Baldinelli Vineyards, 10801 Dickson Rd., Plymouth 95669. 70 acres of vineyards planted to Zinfandel, Cabernet Sauvignon and Sauvignon Blanc, with some 62-year-old vines still producing; 14,000-case capacity. Tasting and tours Sat.-Sun., 11-4, or by appointment. (209) 245-3398.

Beau Val, 10671 Valley Drive (off Bell Rd.), Plymouth 95669. Small, family owned and operated winery, est. 1979. Limited releases of Zinfandel, White Zinfandel and Sauvignon Blanc. Tasting and sales by appointment. (209) 245-3281.

Boeger Winery, 1709 Carson Rd., Placerville 95667. Historic winery, housed in stone cellar built in 1872 and now open to public tours. Offerings include estate bottled Zinfandel, White Zinfandel, Cabernet Sauvignon, Sauvignon Blanc, Chenin Blanc, Merlot, Chardonnay and Johannisberg Riesling. Picnic area on premises. Winery hours: 10-5, Wed.-Sun. (916) 622-8094.

Chapin Vineyards, 12455 Steiner Rd., Plymouth 95669. Small family owned winery, est. 1984; vineyard est. 1976. Wines: Zinfandel, White Zinfandel, Sauvignon Blanc, Burgundy. Tasting room open Sat.-Sun. 10-4, or by appointment. (209) 245-3430.

Chispa Cellars, cnr. French Gulch Rd. and Murphys Grade (at the end of Main St.), Murphys 95247. Winery housed in old barn, est. 1976. Producer of estate Zinfandel. Open Sat.-Sun. 2-5. (209) 728-2106.

D'Agostini Winery, 14430 Shenandoah Rd., Plymouth 95669. Historic winery, originally established in 1856. Some of the original Zinfandel vines are still producing, and the old stone cellar with its collection of fine, hand-crafted oak casks, which also is still in use, is open to public tours. Agostini bottles estate Zinfandel, White Zinfandel, Burgundy, Sauvignon Blanc, and Muscat Canelli; also some sparkling wines are offered. Daily tours and tasting, 10-5; closed major holidays. (209) 245-6612.

Fitzpatrick Winery, 6881 Fairplay Rd., Somerset 95684. Limited releases of Zinfandel, Sauvignon Blanc, Cabernet Sauvignon and Chardonnay, all made from grapes grown in vineyards in El Dorado and Amador counties. Picnic area on premises. Tasting on weekends 11-5, or by appointment; open-house on first weekend in June. (209) 245-3248 or (916) 626-1988.

Gerwer Winery, 8221 Stony Creek Rd. (just off Fairplay Rd.), Somerset 95684. Estate vineyards planted to Ruby Cabernet, Sauvignon Blanc, Petite Sirah and Semillon. Gerwer also makes wines from grapes from other select vineyards in the region. Offerings include White Zinfandel, Chardonnay and Cabernet Sauvignon, primarily. Tasting on Sat. & Sun. 11-5. Oak-

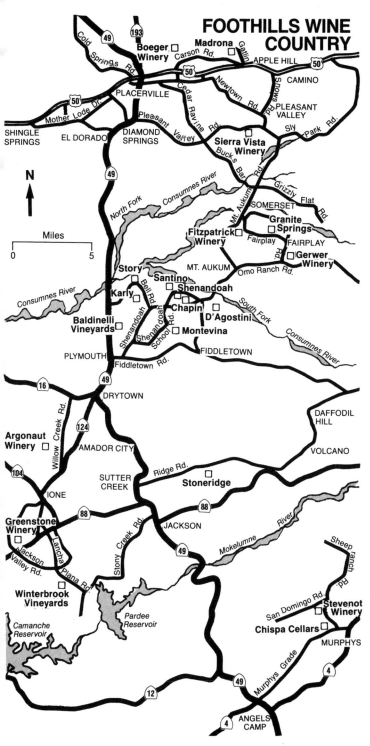

FOOTHILLS WINE COUNTRY

Boeger Winery
Madrona
APPLE HILL
CAMINO
Carson Rd.
Gatlin
Cold Springs Rd.
Newtown Rd.
PLEASANT VALLEY
PLACERVILLE
Cedar Ravine Rd.
Snows Rd.
Mother Lode Dr.
Pleasant Valley Rd.
Sly Park Rd.
SHINGLE SPRINGS
EL DORADO
DIAMOND SPRINGS
Sierra Vista Winery
Buck's Bar Rd.
N
Consumnes River
Grizzly Flat Rd.
North Fork
SOMERSET
Mt Aukum Rd.
Miles
0   5
Fitzpatrick Winery
Granite Springs
FAIRPLAY
Fairplay Rd.
Gerwer Winery
Omo Ranch Rd.
MT. AUKUM
Story
Santino
Consumnes River
Karly
Bell Rd.
Shenandoah
Chapin
South Fork
Baldinelli Vineyards
Shenandoah Rd.
School Rd.
D'Agostini
Montevina
Consumnes River
PLYMOUTH
Fiddletown Rd.
FIDDLETOWN
16
49
DRYTOWN
DAFFODIL HILL
124
Argonaut Winery
Willow Creek Rd.
AMADOR CITY
VOLCANO
104
SUTTER CREEK
Ridge Rd.
Stoneridge
IONE
88
88
JACKSON
Mokelumne River
Greenstone Winery
Stony Creek Rd.
Lancha Plana Rd.
49
Sheep Ranch Rd.
Jackson Valley Rd.
Stevenot Winery
San Domingo Rd.
Winterbrook Vineyards
Pardee Reservoir
Chispa Cellars
MURPHYS
Camanche Reservoir
Murphys Grade
4
12
49
4
ANGELS CAMP

shaded picnic area on premises.(209) 245-3467.

Granite Springs Winery, 6060 Granite Springs Rd. (off Fairplay Rd.), Somerset 95684. Hillside vineyards planted to Zinfandel, Cabernet Sauvignon, Sauvignon Blanc, Chenin Blanc and Petite Sirah. Charming little picnic area by pond. Winery open 11-5 on weekends, or by appointment. (209) 245-6395.

Greenstone Winery, Hwy. 88 and Jackson Valley Rd. (P.O. Box 1164), Ione 95640. Estate bottled Zinfandel. Tree-shaded picnic area. Tasting and tours: 10-4 Wed.-Sun. during July and Aug., 11-4 Sat.-Sun. rest of the year; closed on major holidays. (209) 274-2238.

Harvest Cellars, P.O. Box 548, Murphys 95247. Premium Dry Apple Wine. Tasting at Stevenot Winery in Murphys, or at High Hill Ranch on Carson Rd., Placerville, near Madrona Vineyards. Hours: 11-5 daily, Sept.-Dec. (209) 728-3436.

Herbert Vineyards, P.O. Box 438, Somerset 95684. Lovely hilltop vineyards at 2,400-foot elevation, planted to Zinfandel grapes. Tasting and sales by appointment; call or write for directions and names of retailers carrying their wines. (916) 626-0548.

Karly Wines, just off Bell Rd. (P.O. Box 721), Plymouth 95669. Offerings include estate grown Zinfandel and Sauvignon Blanc, as well as a Chardonnay from grapes grown in the Santa Maria Valley; also small bottlings of experimental varieties. Tasting room open 12-4 Mon.-Fri., 11-4 on weekends. (209) 245-3922.

Kenworthy Vineyards, Shenandoah Rd., Plymouth 95669. Limited releases of Zinfandel, Cabernet Sauvignon and Chardonnay. Open Sun. 12-5, or by appointment. (209) 245-3198.

Lionel W. Richards Winery, P.O. Box 371, Mt. Aukum 95656; located on Perry Creek Rd., 2¼ miles from Gray's Corner in Somerset. Newest winery in the region, first release in spring 1986. Wines: Chardonnay, Cabernet Sauvignon and Chenin Blanc. Call for tasting hours. (916) 443-1905.

Madrona Vineyards, Gatlin Rd. (P.O. Box 454), Camino 95709. Vineyards at 3,000-foot elevation, planted to Zinfandel, Cabernet Sauvignon, Chardonnay, Merlot and Johannisberg Riesling. Estate bottled wines. Hours: Sat. 10-5, Sun. 1-5, or by appointment. (916) 644-5948.

Montevina, 20680 Shenandoah School Rd., Plymouth 95669. Leading producer of Amador County wines; offers premium estate bottled Zinfandel, White Zinfandel, Barbera, Sauvignon Blanc, Cabernet Sauvignon, Chardonnay, Semillon. Tasting and tours daily 11-4; large groups by appointment. (209) 245-6942.

Pigeon Creek Clockspring Vineyards, P.O. Box 355, Plymouth 95669. Varietal Zinfandel and Sauvignon Blanc, made from grapes grown in the estate's 350-acre vineyards at an elevation of 1,600 feet. Tasting and tours by appointment; call or write for directions. (209) 245-3297.

Santino Wines, 12225 Steiner Rd., Plymouth 95669. Zinfandel, White Zinfandel, Cabernet Sauvignon and Sauvignon Blanc are the wines produced here. Tours and tasting Mon.-Fri. 10-4, Sat.-Sun. 12-4. (209) 245-6979.

Shenandoah Vineyards, 12300 Steiner Rd., Plymouth 95669. Small family-owned winery, est. 1977. Maker of estate Zinfandel. Tasting daily 11-5. (209) 245-3698.

Sierra Vista Winery, 4560 Cabernet Way, Placerville 95667; in order to reach the winery, follow Leisure Lane from Pleasant Valley Rd. at Pleasant Valley store. Sierra Vista offers varietal wines primarily, including Zinfandel, White Zinfandel, Cabernet Sauvignon, Fume Blanc, Semillon, and Sirah. Open weekends 11-5, or by appointment. (916) 622-7221.

Stevenot, San Domingo Rd. (P.O. Box 548), Murphys 95247. Winery housed in old hay-barn. Wines produced are Zinfandel, White Zinfandel,

Cabernet Sauvignon, Sauvignon Blanc, Chenin Blanc and Chardonnay. Picnic area on premises. Open daily, 10-5. (209) 728-3436.

Stoneridge, 13862 Ridge Road East, Sutter Creek 95685. Small family winery, est. 1975. Offerings include Zinfandel, White Zinfandel, and Ruby Cabernet. Picnic area on premises. Winery hours: 12-4 Sat.-Sun. (209) 223-1761.

Story Vineyard, 10525 Bell Rd., Plymouth 95669. Small family-owned vineyard estate, est. 1973. Produces primarily white table wines, and an estate grown Zinfandel. Tasting on weekends, or by appointment. (209) 245-6208/245-6827.

Winterbrook Vineyards, 4851 Lancha Plana Rd., Ione 95640. Winery housed in restored 1860s barn. Offers Zinfandel, White Zinfandel, Chenin Blanc, Sauvignon Blanc and Cabernet Sauvignon. Tasting on weekends 11-5, or by appointment. (209) 274-4627.

 RECREATION LAKES. *Lake Amador*, Lake Amador Dr. (off Hwy. 88), south of Ione. Small lake with 400 acres of water and a depth of approximately 50 feet. It is noted primarily for its fishing, especially the record-size black bass. The resort also has boating, camping, a playground, recreation room, restaurant and waterslide. Motorcycles and water-skiing are not permitted at the lake. Day use fee: $3.75; day boat use: $3.50. Limited season. For information call (209) 274-4739.

Pardee Lake, Buena Vista Rd. (off Hwy. 88), 12 miles southwest of Jackson. Reputed fishing lake, with 2,257 acres of water and 37 miles of shoreline; only sail boats and fishing boats allowed on lake. Resort facilities include a campground, marina, bait and tackle shop, laundromat, swimming pool, coffee shop, and trailer park. Also some bird-watching around the lake. Open for a limited season; admission fee charged for day use. For information call (209) 772-1472, or write Pardee Lake Resort, P.O. Box 224B, Ione 95640.

Camanche Lake. Located on the Mokelumne River, just below Pardee Lake, Camanche has 7,722 acres of water, 62 miles of shoreline, and an average depth of around 150 feet. There are two major resorts at the lake: South Camanche Shore and Camanche Northshore Resort. Both have excellent facilities, including marinas with boat ramps, boat rentals, water-skiing, sailing, swimming, beaches, picnicking, horseback riding, campgrounds and trailer parks, rental cottages, boat storage, snack bars, stores and laundromats; the south shore also has a movie amphitheater and a waterslide. Both resorts are open year-round, and charge an admission fee. The South Camanche Shore entrance is off Hwy. 12, near Wallace; for information call (209) 763-5178, or write P.O. Box 92, Wallace 95254. Camanche Northshore Resort is located on Camanche Parkway North (off Hwy. 88), Ione 95640; for information call (209) 763-5121.

New Hogan Lake, off Hwy. 12, 1 mile south of Valley Springs. Recreation area maintained by Corps of Engineers; facilities include a marina with boat ramps, campground, fishing, hiking, picnicking, water-skiing, horse trails, and a nearby store. Also some bird-watching in surrounds. Open year-round, no admission fee. For more information call (209) 772-1343, or write the Corps of Engineers, P.O. Box 128, Valley Springs 95252.

New Melones Reservoir. Situated on the Stanislaus River just below Angels Camp (off Hwy. 49), the lake is 26 miles long, with 100 miles of shoreline and a water capacity of 2.4 million acre-feet; it also has a maximum depth of around 200 feet, upriver, nearer to Parrots Ferry. There are two recreation areas here: to the north of the Hwy. 49 bridge is the Glory Hole Recreation Area, and to the south is the Tuttletown Recreation Area. Facilities include campgrounds, RV parking, picnic areas, restrooms, sandy beaches, and boat ramps. Fishing is also quite promising, with abundant rainbow trout, king and silver salmon, German browns, large mouth bass, crappie, bluegill and catfish. Also, just past the Parrots Ferry bridge at Marble Quarry there is a small family of resident bald eagles, often visible to boaters, and some other wildlife can be seen along the banks, from time to time, as well, including deer, fox, coyote and jackrabbits. New Melones is open year-round.

Tulloch Lake. Located just below New Melones Reservoir, south of Copperopolis, it is reached on O'Byrnes Ferry Rd. which goes off Hwy. 4 at Copperopolis, or off Hwy 108 at the Yosemite Junction. The lake has 55 miles of shoreline and some excellent recreational facilities, including water-skiing, sailing, swimming, fishing, picnicking, a fully-stocked store, and a lodge (Poker Flat Lodge) with well-appointed rooms, a cocktail lounge, dining and banquet rooms, a lakeside bar, and a superb marina. The resort is open year-round, and there is no admission fee. Lodge phone: (209) 785-2286; marina phone: (209) 785-2240.

Lake Don Pedro, Bonds Flat Rd. (off Hwy. 132 and La Grange Rd.), just east of La Grange or west of Coulterville. This is one of the largest lakes in the area, with 150 miles of shoreline, and a host of facilities, including two large campgrounds, a small, adjoining swimming lake, an 18-hole public golf course, houseboat rentals, fishing, boating, picnicking, and a store and laundromat. Open year-round. For more information call (209) 852-2207.

Lake McClure. Situated on the Merced River just southwest of Coulterville, this is also a relatively large lake, one mile long and two miles wide. There are three recreation areas here: McClure Point, Barret Cove and Horseshoe Bend; the first two are situated off Merced Falls Rd. (which intersects Hwy. 132 as well as Hwy. 59), and Horseshoe Bend has an entrance off Hwy. 132, not far from Coulterville. Facilities at the lake include houseboat rentals, camping, bass fishing, water-skiing, marinas, stores, snack bars, and a nearby golf course. The resort is open year-round; day use fee is $3.50. For reservations and information, call (209) 378-2520 or 1-800-468-8889, or write Lake McClure, 9090 Lake McClure Rd., Snelling 95369.

WHITEWATER RAFTING. At least three of the Gold Country's eight major rivers are open to rafting — a summer recreational sport that in recent years has become enormously popular in the foothills. Commercial whitewater guides offer 1 to 3-day trips on these rivers, with overnight adventures featuring wilderness campsites and some delightful outdoor cooking, including pan-baked desserts, reminiscent of the gold rush days. Prices for these guided trips, which are quoted on a per person basis, vary, depending on whether you raft on a weekend or weekday, peak season or off-peak season; on some of the runs discounts of 10%-15% are available to youths (persons under the age of 17).

River Classifications. The American Whitewater Affiliation has established the following classifications, according to the degree of difficulty, for runable whitewater: *Class I* – Very Easy (practised beginners); *Class II* – Easy (intermediate); *Class III* – Moderate (experienced); *Class IV* – Difficult (highly skilled with several years experience with organized group); *Class V* – Very Difficult (teams of experts); *Class VI* – Extremely Difficult (teams of experts).

River Trips. *American River – South Fork*; (Class II-III). One of the favorite whitewater runs in the Gold Country, with at least 25 different sets of rapids, including such memorable ones as the Meat Grinder, Trouble Maker and Old Scary. Last 3 miles are continuous whitewater, with the river rushing past Fowler's Rock and plunging into the American Gorge where one encounters Satan's Cesspool, Hospital Bar and the Emergency Run Rapids. Scenery enroute is quite splendid, and vacationers can be seen panning for gold by the river banks. One-day trips start from Rivers Bend, 2½ miles north of Coloma on Hwy. 49, and end at the Folsom Reservoir, covering a distance of 14 miles; two-day trips begin farther north at Chili Bar, running 21 miles. Cost: one-day $65-$80; two-day $135-$170.

American River Lodge Excursion – Bed & Breakfast Holiday. An optional plan offered on the two-day South Fork run, with overnight accommodation being provided at one of Coloma's historic inns, rather than at a wilderness site. One may select from either the venerable Vineyard House which dates from 1878, or the Coloma Country Inn which is housed in a charming 1850s home. The Bed & Breakfast plan comprises 3 nights accommodation at an inn, one night before the rafting trip, another during the trip and a third after the trip. Cost for the two-day American River Lodge Excurion is $225.00, and for the Bed & Breakfast Holiday, $296.00.

American River – Middle Fork; (Class III). Least crowded and newest section of the American River, this 15-mile run is mostly Class II and III, with the exception of Tunnel Chute (an actual 75-foot tunnel blasted through granite by early day miners) which has Class IV rapids. Scenery along the way is delightful, and modern day miners can be seen with their dredges on the river. These are two-day trips, beginning from just outside Auburn, with the take-out point above the Ruck-A-Chucky Falls. Cost: $185-$195.

American River – North Fork; (Class IV-V). This is one of the faster deep-canyon rivers, not designed for the casual rafter; sudden drops and big holes call for tight manouvering. First 5 miles feature several quite interesting rapids such as the Chamberlain Falls and the Staircase, but during the latter part the river slows to an enjoyable pace, and one can view native wildflowers. Essentially a one-day trip, beginning just outside Auburn (same as for the Middle Fork). Cost: $78-$88.

Tuolumne River; (Class IV). Here is one of the grandest of the Gold Country rivers, with some of the west's most challenging whitewater adventures, and rapids that are rated among the best in the country. Features include the Clavey Falls which have a Class V drop, Sunderland's Chute, Hackamack's Hole, Rams Head, Grey's Grindstone and Hell's Kitchen. The wilderness enroute is quite primitive, interspersed with secluded side streams and delightful sandy beaches that are rich in both the gold mining past and the history of the Miwok Indians. During spring the river banks are awash with wildflowers, and much wildlife can be observed in the surrounding country, including such rare specimens as bald eagles, golden eagles, river otters and ring-tailed cats. Special fishing trips are also available on this stretch in October. 18-mile run, begins at Lumsden, just outside Groveland, and ends at Wards Ferry. Cost: one-day trip $130-$150; two-day trip $240-$265; three-day trip $345-$375.

Upper Tuolumne River – Cherry Creek; (Class V-VI). An expert whitewater run through the steep Jawbone Canyon, noted as one of the most thrilling in the West. Some of the rapids are Class VI, extremely difficult, and one waterfall is portaged. Features include the Horseshoe Falls, Flat Rock Falls, Lewis' Leap and Mushroom. 1½-day 9-mile run, begins at Cherry Creek above Buck Meadows, and ends at Lumsden near Groveland. Cost is $195-$270, depending on the type of raft used.

Merced River; (Class IV & III). The Merced from the famous Yosemite Falls in a thunderous swell, mellowing into a runable river just below El Portal. There are several quite exciting features, including the famed Quarter Mile Rapids and the 20-foot North Fork Falls which must be portaged. The river is ideally suited to paddle boats, twisting and turning through a narrow canyon, following the old Yosemite Railroad part of the way, and passing by several abandoned gold mines. This is a 24-mile run which starts at Cranberry, just above the South Fork of the river, and passes through Split Rock and on to Bagby; the one-day run ends at Split Rock, just 12 miles downriver. Cost: one-day $88-$98; two-day $185-$205.

Whitewater Guides. *O.A.R.S.* (Outdoor Adventure River Specialists), P.O. Box 67, Angels Camp 95222; (209) 736-4677. *Zephyr River Expeditions*, P.O. Box 510, Columbia 95310, (209) 532-6249. *Chili Bar White Water Tours*, 1669 Chili Ct., Placerville 95667; (916) 622-6104. *Sierra Mac River Trips*, P.O. Box 366, Sonora 95370; (209) 532-1327. *Adventure Connection*, P.O. Box 475, Coloma 95613; (916) 626-7385. *California River Trips*, P.O. Box 460, Lotus 95651; (916) 626-8006. *Whitewater Connection*, 7170 Hwy. 49, Lotus 95651; (916) 622-6446. *River Runners*, P.O. Box 433 Coloma 95613; (916) 622-5110. *ABLE Rafting Co.*, 4965 Little Rd., Coloma 95613; (916) 626-6208. *Whitewater Expeditions & Tours*, P.O. Box 160024, Sacramento 95816; (916) 451-3241. *Tuolumne River Expeditions*, P.O. Box 371, Sonora 95370; (209) 532-6113. *Wet n Wild*, P.O. Box 1500, Woodland 95695; (800) 238-3688/(916) 622-5431.

 FISHING. There are several good fishing lakes and rivers in the Mother Lode, blessed with a variety of fish; trout, however, are most common in the high country just east of the foothills, and bass in the lower regions. Fishing licenses can be obtained at one of the Fish and Game Department offices, or from some of the bait and tackle shops; license fee is around $19.00 for California residents, and there is usually a catch limit of 10 fish.

Fishing Areas. *Pardee Lake*; off Hwy. 26, west of Jackson. Commonly found are large-mouth bass, small-mouth bass, crappie, catfish, bluegill, kokanee, and rainbow and brown trout.

Camanche Lake; off Hwy. 12 and Camanche Parkway, west of Jackson. The lake has bass, catfish, bluegill, crappie, sunfish, kokanee and trout.

Lake Amador; off Hwy. 88 and Amador Lake Drive, south of Ione. Mainly large-mouth bass; some trout and kokanee also.

Consumnes River; near River Pines, 7 or 8 miles northeast of Plymouth. Limited trout in spring.

Bear River Lake; off Hwy. 88,, 42 miles east of Jackson. Rainbow trout mainly.

New Hogan Lake; off Hwy. 12, just south of Valley Springs. Bass and catfish; some bluegill, crappie and trout also.

Mokelumne River-Middle Fork; section just above Hwy. 49. Rainbow trout planted annually.

Lake Tulloch; 4 miles northwest of Yosemite Junction (Hwys. 120 and 108). Bass, catfish, crappie; also trout in late spring and summer.

New Melones Reservoir; Hwy. 49, below Angels Camp. Rainbow trout, king and silver salmon, German browns, large-mouth bass, crappie, bluegill and catfish.

White Pines Lake; off Hwy. 4, 1 mile from Arnold. Bass, trout, catfish.

Stanislaus River; near Parrots Ferry Rd. Excellent trout.

Pinecrest Lake; off Hwy. 108, 30 miles northeast of Sonora. Trout mainly.

Lake Don Pedro; off Hwy. 132 and La Grange Rd., northwest of Coulterville. Mainly bass; also some trout and crappie.

Lake McClure; off Hwy. 132 and Merced Falls Rd., southwest of Coulterville. Warm water — large-mouth bass, bluegill, sunfish.

Cherry Lake; located above Tuolumne River, roughly 20 miles north off Hwy. 120 at Bucks Meadow. Mainly trout.

Bass Lake; 10 miles west of Oakhurst, on Road 222 off Hwy. 41. Rainbow trout and fingerling kokanee.

Willow Creek above Bass Lake and *Big Creek* at Fish Camp are also good fishing areas.

Special Fishing Area. *Springfield Trout Farm*; 21980 Springfield Rd. (1 mile southwest of Columbia State Park), Sonora, (209) 532-4623. Pond stocked with Rainbow trout; no license required, and no limit. Open year-round, 10-5.

HUNTING. Deer is the most common game in the foothills, with small populations of bobcats and bear to be found here and there as well. Also waterfowl and resident and migratory birds are abundant. Hunting licenses are around $18.50 for California residents, with additional amounts for the various tags.

For rules, regulations, game limits, and hunting licenses, contact your nearest Fish and Game Department office. Some local sports stores are also able to renew and issue licenses.

HIKING. Several hiking and back-packing opportunities are available in the high country wilderness east of the foothills, with most trails beginning at one or the other of the more primitive campgrounds operated by the Forest Service or P.G.& E., and leading to nearby rivers and lakes. Contact the nearest Forest Service office for information on hiking in these areas.

State parks in the area also offer hiking possibilities. In the *Calaveras Big Trees State Park* roughly 15 miles of trails wind through lush forest growths, with much to interest nature buffs. In the *Indian Grinding Rock* and *Marshall Gold Discovery* state parks there are three or four short, interpretive nature trails meandering through the grounds; these feature historic, cultural and nature exhibits.

Also at some of the lake resorts there are short self-guided hikes which lead to Indian caves and abandoned mine shafts.

HOT-AIR BALLOONING. Hot-air balloon flights are quite enjoyable over the Coloma-Lotus Valley, where you can often see deer grazing in the tranquil surrounds, just back from the American River. Commercial flights are offered by the *Coloma Country Inn* at Coloma, (916) 622-6919; cost for a 35-minute flight is usually around $125.00 per person. The inn also offers a ballooning-bed and breakfast package for $165.00 per person per night. Call the inn for more information. Also, *O.A.R.S.* offers ballooning-rafting packages, with overnight accommodation at the Coloma Country Inn; cost for the package is $235.00 during the week and $255.00 on weekends. For reservations and information, call (209) 736-4677, or write O.A.R.S., P.O. Box 67, Angels Camp 95222.

GOLF. *Sierra Golf Course*, 1822 Country Club Dr., Placerville; (916) 622-0760. 9-hole course with pro shop. Open year-round.

La Contenta Golf & Country Club, 1653 Hwy. 26, Valley Springs; (209) 772-1081. 18-hole course; facilities include driving range, putting green, pro shop, golf carts, lessons.

Meadowmont Golf Course, 1684 Hwy. 4, Arnold; (209) 795-1313. 9-hole, 36-par course; pro shop, rentals, lessons.

Sequoia Woods Country Club, Cypress Point Dr., Arnold; (209) 795-2141. 18 holes, pro shop, golf carts, restaurant and lounge.

Phoenix Lake Golf Club, 21448 Paseo De Los Portales (4 miles out on Phoenix Lake Rd.), Sonora; (209) 532-0111. 9 holes, driving range, lessons, pro shop, snack bar. Open year-round.

Twain Harte Golf Club, Twain Harte Dr., Twain Harte; (209) 586-3131. 9-hole course; pro shop.

Sierra Pines Golf Course, South Fork Rd., Twain Harte; (209) 586-2118. 9 holes, pro shop, golf carts.

Forest Meadows Golf Course, Hwy. 4 (3 miles east of Murphys), Murphys; (209) 728-3439. 18-hole, Robert Trent-designed course; pro shop, lessons.

Lake Don Pedro Golf & Country Club, Bonds Flat Rd. (off Hwy. 132 and La Grange Rd.), La Grange; (209) 852-2242. 18-hole course; pro shop, golf carts, lessons.

Pine Mountain Lake Golf Course, off Hwy. 120, near Groveland (26 miles west of Yosemite); (209) 962-7471. 18-hole course; pro shop, golf carts, lessons.

Sierra Sky Ranch and Golf Course, 50552 Road 632, Oakhurst; (209) 683-4433. 9-hole, 3,155-yard course; pro shop, golf carts, bar.

 BICYCLING. There are some quite enchanting side roads off Highway 49 which provide cycling enthusiasts with excellent opportunities. Central Gold Country, in particular Amador County, is especially favored for its small country roads which are mostly in good repair and experience very little motor traffic. The Shenandoah and Jackson valleys, and around Buena Vista (some miles to the west of Jackson) and the Camanche, Pardee and Amador lakes, are good areas for bicycling.

Bike Routes. *Jackson-Pardee Lake.* The 9-mile route from Jackson to Pardee Lake, along Stoney Creek Road (west off Hwy. 49), will treat you to some lovely rolling countryside and a variety of foliage; there are some ancient stone walls to be seen alongside the road as well. The road is quite winding but otherwise in good repair, and at Pardee Lake there is a store and picnic area.

Plymouth-River Pines-Fiddletown is another worthwhile cycling route, leading throuth the fertile Shenandoah Valley where several vineyards can be visited. From Plymouth take Route E-16 to River Pines, passing by the historic D'Agostini Winery which has a picnic area and wine tasting facilities. From River Pines travel south on Lawrence Road and Fiddletown-Tyler Road to the tiny tree-shaded village of Fiddletown, where there is an 1850s store and a recreation park with picnic tables. From Fiddletown return to Plymouth on the Fiddletown Road which is quite narrow and with some interesting scenery. The entire trip is 17-18 miles, and takes more or less a full day.

Sutter Creek-Volcano-Sutter Creek. One of the most popular designated bike routes is "The Loop" — Sutter Creek-Volcano-Indian Grinding Rock State Park-Pine Grove, then on to Jackson and back to Sutter Creek — a 28-mile round trip. The first 12-mile section, from Sutter Creek to the picturesque mountain town of Volcano, is uphill, with the road winding through wooded areas and across open fields, following alongside a creek much of the way. From Volcano it is 1½ miles to the Indian Grinding Rock State Park which has a picnic area, and another 2 miles to Pine Grove where there is a bike rest at the Pine Grove Park. From Pine Grove take Ridge Road and New York Ranch Road, 10 or 11 miles downhill, to Jackson; then return to Sutter Creek, 2 miles north, by way of either Highway 49 or Jackson Gate Road and Highway 49.

Southern Gold Country   **89**

Glencoe-Mountain Ranch. 9 miles to the west of Mokelumne Hill, on Highway 26, is Glencoe, from where one can cycle some 14 miles southwest on Mountain Ranch Road to Mountain Ranch; the terrain is gentle, the countryside quite scenic, and the roads are in good repair, with light traffic.

Several other side roads in the area can be enjoyed on a bicycle as well, but always plan your route well ahead, for the varied foothills terrain can sometimes be quite treacherous, especially on hot summer days.

Also, bicycle clubs affiliated with the Sierra Club or other organizations such as the American Youth Hostels, conduct bike tours through the Sierra foothills, though these follow a more rigorous schedule, usually taking in 40 to 50 miles in a day.

HORSEBACK RIDING. *Sugar Creek Boarding Stables*, 2701 Birch Ave., Camino (east of Placerville on Hwy. 50); (916) 644-6825. Scenic trail rides through National Forest; lessons. Call for directions to stables.

Shadow Glen Riding Stables, 4854 Main Ave., Fair Oaks, (west of Placerville); (916) 989-1826. Scenic trail rides, lakeshore riding, lessons, moonlight and day rides. Group rates available.

Camanche Northshore Resort Stables, Camanche Parkway North, off Hwy. 88 (west from Jackson); (209) 763-5295. Horse rentals and trail rides.

Columbia Stable, Main St. (at Wells Fargo Express Office), Columbia. Trail rides through Columbia's back country. Half-hour ride $8.00, one-hour ride $15.00, two-hour ride $25.00. For reservations and information call (209) 785-2263 or (209) 785-2244.

Yosemite Trails Pack Station, at Fish Camp (12 miles northeast of Oakhurst); (209) 683-7611. Scenic trails, 2-hour guided loop trails, rides to giant sequoia grove in Yosemite National Park; also lessons. Open daily in summer.

SKIING. Downhill Ski Areas. *Dodge Ridge*, Dodge Ridge Rd. (off Hwy. 108), Pinecrest. This is one of the largest ski resorts in the area; facilities include chair lifts, NASTAR races, lessons, ski rentals. For information call (209) 965-3474, or write Dodge Ridge, P.O. Box 1188, Pinecrest 95364.

Mt. Reba Ski Area, Mount Reba Rd. (off Hwy. 4), Bear Valley. 7 double chair lifts, 2,100 ft. vertical, lessons, ski rentals. For information call (209) 753-2301.

Cross-country Ski Areas. *Bear River Lake Resort*, Hwy. 88 (42 miles east of Jackson), Pioneer. Cross-country skiing, snowmobiling, sleigh rides, and sleds; some equipment rentals. Lodging and snack bar. For information and reservations call (209) 295-4868.

Cottage Springs Ski & Play Area, cnr. Hwy. 4 and Beatrice Dr., Camp Connell. Cross-country skiing, sleds, ski rentals; general store at camp. For information call (209) 795-1209.

Calaveras Big Trees State Park, Hwy .4, Arnold. Wilderness cross-country skiing and snowshoeing along marked trails. Park phone: (209) 795-2334.

Tamarack, Hwy. 4, a few miles west of Bear Valley. Cross-country skiing; ski rentals available.

CAMPGROUNDS AND RV PARKS. There is an abundance of campgrounds and RV parks in the Mother Lode, with at least a dozen or so along major highways and several others at the area's many lakes; facilities range from the usual campground restrooms, showers, piped water and RV hookups, to fishing, boating, swimming, water-skiing, hiking, and horseback riding. In addition, there is a profusion of wilderness campsites along Highways 88, 4, 108 and 120, available mainly through the Forest Service; for information on these, contact the nearest Forest Service office, or the local chamber of commerce.

Following is a selective list of developed campgrounds and RV parks, with facilities.

In the **Placerville-Coloma Area**. *Camp Chiquita*, Wentworth Springs Rd. (7 miles east of Georgetown), Georgetown; (916) 333-4673. Camping facilities available during season. Camping fee: $7.00-$12.00.

Camp Coloma, Hwy. 49 (P.O. Box 11), Coloma 95613; (916) 622-6700. Camping, rental cabins and cottages, swimming pool, children's playground, rafting, gold panning lessons, store, restaurant. Closed Nov.-March. Camping fee: $10.00-$17.00.

Camp Lotus, 5461 Bassi Rd., Lotus 95651; (916) 622-8672. Camping, rafting, fishing, picnicking, gold panning, showers, restrooms. Camping fee: $6.00-$10.00.

Coloma Resort, 6921 Mt. Murphy Rd. (P.O. Box 186, Coloma 95613; (916) 622-5799. Camping, full-hookups for RVs, showers, restrooms, gas station, store, fishing, swimming, rafting. Camping fee: $10.00-$12.00.

Ponderosa Park Campground. Hwy. 49 (at the South Fork of the American River), Coloma 95613; (916) 622-9849. Membership campground with camping, full-hookups for RVs, propane, store, fishing, rafting, kayaking, swimming. Non-members on space-available basis. Camping fee: $15.00.

In the **Jackson-Plymouth Area**. *Camanche Northshore Resort*, Camanche Parkway North, Ione 95640; (209) 763-5121. Primitive campground with 400 campsites, spaces for RVs (any length), showers, fishing, boating, water-skiing, horseback riding, playground, store and snack bar; also rentals of motel cottages, patio boats, sail boats, and beach rentals. Camping fee: $12.00 per vehicle for 2 persons, additional $1.00. Reservations recommended.

Far Horizons 49er Trailer Village, cnr. Hwy. 49 and Empire St. (P.O. Box 191), Plymouth 95669; (209) 245-6981. Complete RV resort with 329 RV spaces with full hookups for 40-foot RVs, 15 pull-through spaces; also showers, laundry, store, food, swimming pools, jacuzzi, recreation halls, pool room, shuffleboard courts, and horseshoe pits. Camping fee: $17.00-$22.00 for 2 persons, additional $2.00. Reservations suggested.

Lake Amador Resort, Lake Amador Drive, Ione; (209) 274-2625. 150 RV spaces (30 with electrical and 50 with water hookups), 20 pull through spaces for 35-foot RVs; also campsites, showers, flush toilets, fishing, swimming, waterslides, playgrounds, recreation area with pool tables, store. Camping fee: $10.00 for up to 5 persons; day use $3.75; day boat use $3.50.

Pardee Lake Resort, Rt. 1 (P.O. Box 224B), Ione 95640 (approach via Buena Vista Rd. from Jackson); (209) 772-1472. 237 spaces for 33-foot RVs (90 spaces with full hookups, 100 with water), 150 campsites; other facilities include swimming pool, boating, fishing, coffee shop, laundry, showers. Camping fee: $7.00-$12.00. Reservations for hookups.

Roaring Camp Mining Co., off Hwy. 88 east (P.O. Box 278), Pine Grove 95665; (209) 296-4100. Historic 49er camp with prospectors' cabins for rent; also guided tours, cookout dinners, gold panning, fishing and swimming. Cabin rental (by the week): $280.00 for 2 persons, $65.00-$105.00 for each additional person.

South Camanche Shore, off Hwy. 12 (P.O. Box 92), Wallace 95254; (209) 763-5178. 168 spaces with full hookups for 35-foot RVs, 600 campsites, showers, laundromat, swimming, boating, fishing, waterslide, horseback riding, store, snack bar, game room; also boat rentals, cottage rentals, amphitheater for movies in summer, and mobile home park. Campsites $12.00, RV spaces $16.00. Reservations suggested for hookup spaces.

Indian Grinding Rock State Historic Park, 1½ miles north of Pine Grove on the Pine Grove-Volcano Rd. (off Hwy. 88); (209) 296-7488. 21 campsites with picnic tables and stoves; also self-guided tours of Miwok Indian village and cultural center. Camping fee: $10.00. Campsites available on first-come first-served basis; reservations through Ticketron.

Bear River Lake Resort, Hwy. 88 (42 miles east of Jackson), Pioneer 95666; (209) 295-4868. 127 wooded campsites, swimming, boating, fishing, hunting, canoeing, water-skiing, hiking, picnicking, recreational sports, snowmobiling and cross-country skiing in winter; also gasoline and propane, store, laundromat, post office, and boat rentals. Camping fee: $10.00-$15.50.

In the **Angels Camp-Arnold Area**. *New Hogan Lake*, off Hwy. 12 (P.O. Box 128), Valley Springs 95252; (209) 772-1343. This is a Corps of Engineers recreation area; facilities include 121 developed campsites, fishing, hiking, boating, picnicking, water-skiing, horse trails, bird watching, and showers.

Calaveras Big Trees State Park, Hwy. 4 (P.O. Box 120), Arnold 95223; (209) 795-2334. 129 developed campsites at 5000-foot elevation, with hot showers and piped water; also picnicking, swimming and fishing in nearby Stanislaus River and Bear Creek, hiking and cross-country skiing and snowshoeing in winter. Camper vehicles permitted during winter season for overnight in parking area. Camping fee: $10.00. Reservations through Ticketron.

Golden Torch RV Resort & Campground, Golden Torch Drive (off Hwy. 4, just above entrance to Calaveras Big Trees State Park), Arnold; (209) 795-2820. Campsites, full hookups for RVs, hot showers, swimming pool, laundromat. Camping fee: $9.00-$16.00.

In the **Sonora-Columbia Area**. *49er Trailer Ranch*, 23223 Italian Bar Rd. (adjacent to state park), Columbia 95310; (209) 532-9898. 40 RV spaces (11 with full hookups), 2 pull-through spaces for 40-foot RVs; also showers, fishing, rafting, gold panning, horseback riding, snow sports, historic tours, square dancing, recreational games, including horseshoes and ping pong. Store and laundromat on premises. Camping fee: $13.50. Reservations suggested.

Marble Quarry RV Resort, 11551 Yankee Hill Rd. (P.O. Box 850), Columbia 95310; (209) 532-9539. 20 RV spaces with full hookups, 60 spaces with water and electrical hookups and dump station, 10 pull-through spaces for 35-foot RVs; also 15 campsites, pool, hiking, store, laundromat, and lounge. Camping fee: $13.75-$18.75. Reservations recommended.

Don Pedro Reservoir, Bonds Flat Rd. (off Hwy. 132 and La Grange Rd.), La Grange 95329; (209) 852-2207. 2 large campgrounds, with barbeque pits, picnic tables and showers; other facilities include a small swimming lake, store, laundromat, houseboat rentals, boating, golf course, and bar. Camping fee: $7.00-$10.00.

River Ranch Campground, Cottonwood Rd. (at Basin Creek), Tuolumne 95379; (209) 928-3708. Facilities include hot showers, piped water and picnic tables. Camping fee: $10.00.

Sugar Pine RV Resort, Hwy. 108, Sugar Pine; (209) 586-4631. RV spaces. Camping fee: $14.00.

In the **Mariposa-Coulterville Area**. *Lake McClure*, 9090 McClure Rd., Snelling 95369; information (209) 378-2520, reservations 1-800-468-8889. The lake has 3 different recreation areas with campgrounds and other facilities. *McClure Point*, Lake McClure Access Rd. (off Merced Falls Rd. which goes off Hwy. 132), Snelling; (209) 378-2521; 100 camping units, 27 RV spaces with water and electrical hookups, hot showers, swimming, boating, water-skiing, fishing, picnicking, houseboat rentals, patio and fishing boat rentals, store, snack bar, laundromat, gasoline supplies. *Barret Cove*, off Merced Falls Rd. (3 miles south from Hwy. 132), La Grange; (209) 378-2711; 275 camping units, 42 RV spaces with water and electrical hookups, hot showers, swimming, boating, water-skiing, fishing, picnicking, houseboat rentals, patio and fishing boat rentals, store, snack bar, laundromat, gasoline supplies; also golf course nearby. *Horseshoe Bend*, 4240 Hwy. 132, Coulterville; (209) 878-3452; 110 camping units, 40 RV spaces with water and electrical hookups, hot showers, swimming, boating, water-skiing, fishing, picnicking, snack bar, store, laundromat, gasoline, houseboat rentals, patio and fishing boat rentals. Camping fee: $9.00-$11.00.

In the **Oakhurst-Bass Lake Area**. *Bass Lake* (10 miles from Oakhurst) has five U.S. Forest Service campgrounds, with a total of nearly 150 units. Reservations are through Ticketron, or through the Bass Lake Recreation Office, located across Road 222 from Recreation Point; phone (209) 642-3212. Camping fees are $9.00 for single units, one vehicle and 6 persons.

Also *Ducey's Resort* at the northern end of Bass Lake has RV spaces.

Fish Camp and *Sugar Pine*, both northeast of Oakhurst, also have campgrounds.

STATE HISTORIC PARKS. Marshall Gold Discovery State Historic Park, Hwy. 49, Coloma (8 miles north of Placerville, or 19 miles south of Auburn). 280-acre gold discovery theme park situated on the South Fork of the American River, comprising roughly 70% of the tiny township of Coloma. Main attraction here is a replica of historic *Sutters Mill*, with hand-hewn beams and mortise-and-tenon joints, which can be seen working on weekends. A couple of short, self-guided walking trails meander through the park — one down to the river where a plaque marks the original *Gold Discovery Site*, and another to the *Marshall Monument* on a hill above town where a 10-foot bronze statue of James Marshall points to the site of the discovery down below. A variety of mining exhibits and gold rush buildings are scattered throughout the park, and two charming 1860s churches stand on Church Street high above town. The park also has a museum, and several picnicking possibilities. There is no camping available within the park, and gold panning in the park section of the American River is prohibited. The park is open daily, 8 a.m. until sunset; museum hours are 10-5. Day use fee: $3.00 per car. For more information call (916) 622-3470, or write *Marshall Gold Discovery State Historic Park*, P.O. Box 265, Coloma 95613.

Indian Grinding Rock State Historic Park, Pine Grove-Volcano Rd. (1½ miles north of Hwy. 88 east at Pine Grove). This is a 136-acre park centered around the Miwok Indian culture, with a real Miwok village and roundhouse, and a cultural center with displays of Indian baskets, weavings, jewelry and tools. Chief attraction is the great *Indian Grinding Rock*, largest of its kind in America (with a replica of it on display at the Smithsonian

Institute in Washington, D.C.), featuring 1,185 mortar holes, once used for grinding nuts and seeds, and 365 petroglyph designs. Campsites with stoves and picnic tables are available at the park. The park is open daily, 8 a.m.-sunset, and the cultural center is open weekends 10-5; park fee is $3.00. For more information call (209) 296-7488.

Calaveras Big Trees State Park, Hwy. 4, 4 miles northeast of Arnold. 5,994-acre park at 4,700-foot elevation, centered around two groves of 13,00-year-old *Giant Sequoias*, some of them 300 feet tall with trunks that measure 30 feet in diameter nearer to the base, and barks that are 8-10 inches thick, often 2 feet thick, An estimated 250,000 tourists visit the park's two groves, the *North Grove* and the *South Grove*, annually. The *North Grove* has some excellent exhibits, including a 25-foot-diameter stump which was once used as a dance floor, and sections of a felled "Mother-of-the-Forest" tree. The *South Grove* is more primitive, lying on the edge of the Stanislaus Forest wilderness, and reached by way of a foot trail into the forest. Camping is available at the park, and there is an interpretive center open during park hours. In winter snowshoeing and cross-country skiing are quite popular here. The park is open daily in summer (June-Sept.), and on weekends the rest of the year; park admission is $3.00 per car. For more information call the park's area office on (209) 795-2334 during regular business hours.

Columbia State Historic Park, Parrots Ferry Rd. (off Hwy. 49), 3 miles north of Sonora. 273-acre park, established in 1945, comprising a restored gold rush town that produced over $87 million in gold within a one-square-mile area. The town has splendid, tree-shaded streets, lined with gold rush era frame cottages and iron-shuttered brick buildings, some restored, others reconstructed to duplicate the originals. Most buildings house gift and antique shops, specialty stores and quaint restaurants, and in summer a tent city at the edge of town recreates the gold rush days, with merchants portraying 19th century pioneers. An array of gold rush exhibits, historic gardens, museums, stagecoach rides, mine tours, gold panning, and a variety of entertainment, including street juggling acts and traveling fiddlers, can also be enjoyed at the park. Also, nearby Columbia Airport offers scenic and commuter flights. There are no camping facilities on the park premises, though bed and breakfast and motel accommodations are available, and a couple of good RV parks can be found just outside the park. The Columbia State Park is open daily, 8 a.m. until sunset; stores are open during business hours. For more information on the park call (209) 532-0150, or write *Columbia State Historic Park*, P.O. Box 151, Columbia 95310.

Railtown 1897 State Historic Park, 5th Ave., Jamestown. Established in 1983, the park is home to the historic *Sierra Railroad* and 26-acre roundhouse, both dating from 1897. The park is also the setting for several Hollywood movies and TV films, including "High Noon" (1952) starring Gary Cooper, and "The Gambler" starring Kenny Rogers. A gift shop, dining car, and picnic grounds are available on the premises, and roundhouse tours and rail excursions on steam locomotives are offered on weekends in summer. (See also *Sierra Railway* in the *Historic Railroads and Tours* section.) For more information on Railtown, call (209) 984-3953.

 THEATER. The Gold Country has a fine history of theater entertainment, going back to the days of the gold rush. Performances are held mainly during the summer months, with a splendid variety offered in melodrama and comedy. Ticket prices usually range from $6.00 to $12.00, depending on the performance.

Area Theaters. *The Olde Coloma Theatre*, Monument Drive, Coloma. Melodrama on weekends, May to September. Reservations recommended. For tickets and information, call (916) 626-5282, or write The Olde Coloma Theatre, P.O. Box 472, Coloma 95613.

The Discovery Playhouse, El Dorado County Fairgrounds, Placerville; (916) 626-3063. Drama during spring and summer.

The Claypipers, at the Piper Playhouse on Hwy. 49, Drytown. Oldest performing group in Mother Lode; melodrama and olios, mid-May through September; Saturday night performances. Reservations required. Call (209) 245-3812, or write The Drytown Club, Drytown 95699.

Pickadilly Players, at the Piper Playhouse on Hwy. 49, Drytown. Contemporary comedy; Friday and Saturday evenings, Jan.-Feb. and Oct.-Nov. Call for program information and reservations: (209) 245-6441 or (209) 245-3812.

Volcano Pioneers Community Theatre Group, at the Cobblestone Theatre on Main St., Volcano. Comedies on weekends, May to October. Small theater with limited seating; call for reservations: (209) 296-4696, or (209) 223-0587.

Black Bart Players, Murphys. Comedy and farces; Saturday night performances, April and November. For reservations and information, write Black Bart Players, P.O. Box 104, Murphys 95247.

The University of the Pacific Repertory, Fallon House Theatre, Columbia State Park. Air-conditioned theater in historic building. Summer performances, evenings and matinees, Tues.-Sun. For information and reservations, call (209) 532-4644, or write Fallon House Theatre, P.O. Box 543, Columbia 95310.

Sierra Repertory Theatre, Mono Way, Sonora. Drama, mystery, musicals; year-round performances, evenings and matinees, Thurs.-Sun. Discounts for children and seniors. For program information and reservations, call (209) 532-3120, or write Sierra Repertory Theatre, P.O. Box 3030, Sonora 95370.

The Golden Chain Theatre, Oakhurst. Summer melodrama and comedies, Friday and Saturday nights. Reservations advised. For tickets and program information, call (209) 683-7112, or write The Golden Chain Theatre, P.O. Box 604, Oakhurst 93644.

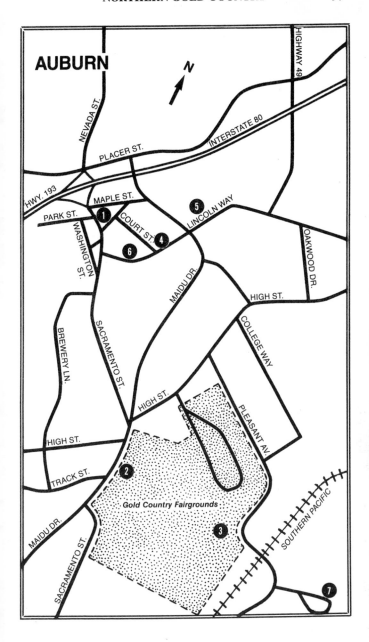

Points of Interest -
1) Old Town
2) Barnhard Winery (1874)
3) Placer County Museum
4) Placer County Courthouse
   (1894)
5) St. Lukes Episcopal
   Church (1862)
6) Brye Mansion (1887)
7) Auburn Dam Overlook

displays. The area produced over $10 million in gold.

Nearby, also of interest, are the old gold camps of Yankee Jim and Michigan Bluff. Michigan Bluff has an historic cemetery, and associations with Leland Stanford, later Governor of California and railroad magnate, who operated a store here during the early 1850s. Michigan Bluff was a notable hydraulicking town, which produced in excess of $6 million in gold between 1853 and 1858 alone; scarred mountain-sides, reminders of the hydraulicking era, can still be seen here.

Colfax to Dutch Flat

Some 12 miles east of Auburn on Interstate 80 is Colfax, originally founded in 1849, but which became important only in 1865, as a railroad town. It is named for Schuyler Colfax, Speaker of the House of Representatives and Vice President under Ulysses S. Grant. The town has one or two railroad displays at its rail terminal, and some ancient buildings in its old town, mostly two and three stories high, including an I.O.O.F. Hall dating from the 1850s.

From Colfax it is possible to journey north to Grass Valley (15 miles) on Highway 174, the oldest road in the county, twisty and beautifully shaded by age-old trees, which also has one or two added attractions — such as a mushroom farm, and Rollins Lake which has good camping, picnicking, swimming and boating opportunities. Also, there is a wild sort of road branching from the highway, which dashes off northeast to the long-forgotten gold camps of Red Dog and You Bet, both hydraulicking centers.

In any case, for the purposes of our tour let us continue east from Colfax on Interstate 80, to Iowa Hill, Gold Run and Dutch Flat. The first of these, Iowa Hill, is reached on a small side road, east off Interstate 80, 6 or 7 miles in. It is a town that was established in 1853 but has been largely destroyed by a series of major fires, the last in 1922. The town nevertheless produced in excess of $20 million in gold, and we are told that prospectors, to this day, continue to find large gold nuggets in the river — the North Fork of the American — just out from town. There is an historic cemetery worth visiting here.

Farther on Interstate 80 is Gold Run, once a substantial town and a center of hydraulic mining, but which now has little of historic note, except an old church. There is, however, a vista point just above town, off the interstate highway, which offers sweeping views of the great wooded valleys of the area.

Almost directly opposite Gold Run is Dutch Flat, which, in contrast, has much that is of historic interest. This is, in fact, one of the only towns in the Gold Country not to have suffered a major fire. In beautiful settings, here are to be seen several charming 19th-century frame buildings such as the Masonic Hall (1856), I.O.O.F. Hall (1852), the two-story Dutch Flat Hotel (1852), the steepled Methodist Episcopal Church (1859), and the delightful schoolhouse which sits on the site of the first cabin ever built at Dutch Flat. There are also dozens of well-preserved homes here, with tin roofs, and a native-stone general store, dating from 1854. Although an hydraulicking town, which peaked in the 1870s, Dutch Flat, more importantly, lies on the transcontinental railroad route.

GRASS VALLEY - NEVADA CITY

There are three highways converging in on Grass Valley — Highway 49 from Auburn (25 miles), Highway 174 from Colfax, and Highway 20 from Rough and Ready, Penn Valley, and Marysville and Yuba City farther west. Directly above Grass Valley lies Nevada City, the other principal town of this area (which is made up wholly of the Nevada County). The area also has in it the famous Malakoff Diggins, North Bloomfield, Washington, Rough and Ready and North San Juan.

Grass Valley

The most famous of all places to visit at Grass Valley is the Empire Mine State Historic Park, a fabulous 784-acre mine estate — acquired by the state in 1975 for a reported $1.25 million — located on Empire Street, just to the southeast of town. Here is the largest, deepest and richest hardrock gold mine in all California, which in its 107 years of operation (1850-1957) produced an estimated $70 million in gold ($960 million at the 1974 world gold prices), spawning a network of some 360 miles of underground mine workings, and reaching a depth of over 11,000 feet on the incline — well below sea level. The mine's vast surface works, including some impressive mine buildings, two headframes and several pieces of old mining equipment, can be seen by the public on guided tours conducted by park personnel, daily in summer and on weekends in spring and fall. Part of the mine's main shaft can also be viewed here, illuminated for some 150 feet.

The great showpiece of the park is of course the Bourne Cottage, an exceptionally lovely stone and brick home, designed by noted San Francisco architect Willis Polk, and set on beautifully-kept grounds with a fountain pool and rose garden. The cottage dates from 1890 and was formerly the summer residence of William Bourne, Jr., the notably wealthy owner of the Empire Mine. (We are reminded that Bourne also built the famous Filoli — which derives from his motto, "Fight, Love, Live" — Mansion at Woodside, California, featured in TV's *Dynasty*.) Be sure, too, to visit the park's small but interesting interpretive center, with its excellent recount of the history of the Empire Mine, including the story of William Bourne and the role played by the Cornish miners in the development of the mine. The Cornish, in fact, were instrumental not only in the success of the Empire Mine, but were a great influence on Grass Valley as a whole. Originally brought over from England's Cornwall district for their skills and knowledge of hardrock mining, they comprised nearly 85% of Grass Valley's population at one time. Their customs and traditions linger to this day, much a part of Grass Valley. Tales of Tommy Knockers, the mythical elfs of mischief (Cornish in origin), are still told with great fondness by the town's old timers, and the delectable Cornish pasty, beloved of local residents, is served at most area res-

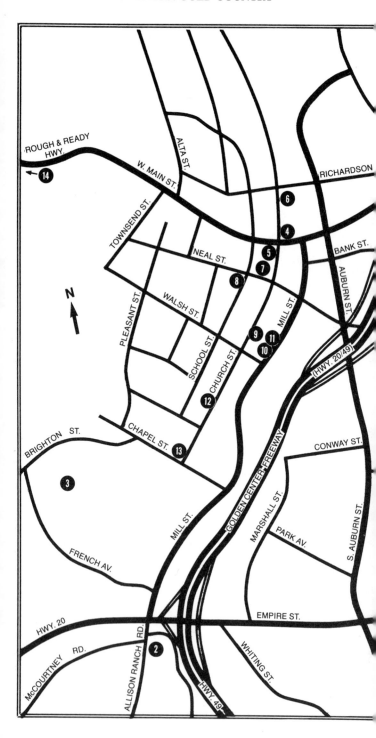

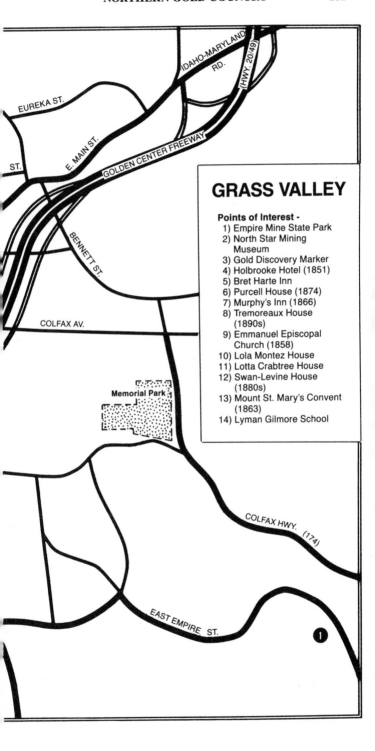

GRASS VALLEY

Points of Interest -
1) Empire Mine State Park
2) North Star Mining Museum
3) Gold Discovery Marker
4) Holbrooke Hotel (1851)
5) Bret Harte Inn
6) Purcell House (1874)
7) Murphy's Inn (1866)
8) Tremoreaux House (1890s)
9) Emmanuel Episcopal Church (1858)
10) Lola Montez House
11) Lotta Crabtree House
12) Swan-Levine House (1880s)
13) Mount St. Mary's Convent (1863)
14) Lyman Gilmore School

taurants. The single most important contribution of the Cornish to Grass Valley's hardrock mining industry, however, was the invaluable Cornish Pump — an ingenious invention involving a series of water-pumps at different levels, with the ability to pump water from incredible depths — which made it possible for the area's mines to mine at these unprecedented depths.

Grass Valley's other notable mines are the North Star, Idaho-Maryland, Pennsylvannia, Golden Center and New Brunswick, and the town itself is honeycombed with hundreds of miles of underground tunnels and shafts, many of them interconnecting. At the southwestern end of town on Allison Ranch Road, one can tour the North Star Mine's power-house, an attractive stone building which now houses the Nevada County Historical Museum. It is considered to be one of the finest mining museums in the West, with several very interesting displays, including a Cornish Pump, a working 20-stamp mill, and a huge Pelton Wheel, 30 feet in diameter, believed to be the largest wheel of its kind in the world. The Pelton Wheel, as such, was originally developed in 1878, as a greatly improved version of the traditional waterwheel, but based on the same principle — water driven. Its main feature was a radically new cast-iron bucket with a center ridge, designed such that when the jet-stream of water struck the bucket to drive the wheel forward, the water was split along the ridge and deflected to the sides, rather than rebounding onto the back to the next bucket; this in turn reduced friction and made the wheel considerably more power-efficient. The wheel on display here, built in 1896, is said to have generated some 1,000 horsepower, turning at the rate of 60 revolutions per minute (70 miles per hour); it supplied the North Star Mine with much of its power needs. Directly below the power-house lies a pleasant little picnic area, delightfully shaded by splendid trees and bordered by the enchanting Wolf Creek — the source of water for North Star's Pelton Wheel.

A little way to the north of the North Star Museum, on a small hill off Jenkins Street, a plaque marks the site of the original quartz-gold discovery at Grass Valley in 1850. And, believe it or not, this is how it came about: a pioneer farmer named George McKnight was out chasing his runaway cow on a moonlit night when he stubbed his toe on a rock outcropping; the rock came loose and revealed what was surely gold — and McKnight forgot all about his cow. He later sold his claim to the Gold Hill Mining Company, which operated here from 1850 to 1857, producing in excess of $4 million in gold.

The Grass Valley township is also not without interest. It contains a wealth of lovely homes, inns and other historically important buildings, the finest being the Holbrooke Hotel on Main Street, dating from 1851 and recently restored to its former elegance. In its infancy it was host to several early-day personages, such as Mark Twain, and Presidents Grant, Garfield, Cleveland and Harrison. Not far from the Holbrooke is the old Bret Harte Inn, dating from 1917; during the early 1900s, it was one of Grass Valley's premier hotels.

On Mill Street stands one of the great landmarks of Grass Valley: the old home of Lola Montez, the frequently glamorous singer, dancer, enchantress, and mistress of King Ludwig of Bavaria, who lived here briefly, 1852 to 1853. The frame home, recently restored, now houses the Grass Valley Chamber of Commerce. Quite close, is also the former home of Lotta Crabtree, America's first entertainer-millionaire, and one-time pupil of Lola Montez. Other historically interesting homes here are the Tremoureaux and Matteson residences on Neal Street, both dating from the 1890s; the Swan-Levine House, a lovely Queen Anne Victorian dating from the 1880s, which formerly was a hospital and is now a bed and breakfast inn, located on Church Street; the Purcell House (1874), also on Church Street; and the ivy-covered Coleman House on Neal Street, built in 1866 by gold baron Edward Coleman, owner of the Idaho-Maryland and North Star mines. This last is now also a bed and breakfast establishment, Murphy's Inn.

Also see the charming wood-frame Emmanuel Episcopal Church on Church Street, dating from 1858 and said to be the oldest Episcopal Church in the Northern Gold Country area; and the St. Jospeh's Chapel (1894) and Mount St. Mary's Convent (1863), both on Church Street, near Chapel. The convent building now houses a museum, open to public. Another point of interest, farther to the north on Highway 20, is the Lyman Gilmore School, notable as the site of the first commercial airfield in the United States. It was here that Lyman Gilmore, pioneer aviator, is believed to have test-flown a 32-foot-span monoplane, powered by a 20-horsepower steam engine, in May of 1902 — a year before the historic flight of the Wright Brothers at Kitty Hawk, North Carolina!

Rough and Ready, French Corral and San Juan

Rough and Ready, lying 5 miles west of Grass Valley on Highway 20, is a small, historic town which, notably, seceded from the Union for some months in 1850, in protest over a miners' tax. It is named for General Zachary Taylor, 12th President of the United States, also known as "Old Rough and Ready." Of historical note in town are an old I.O.O.F. Hall, a wood-frame toll house, and the W.H. Fippin Blacksmith Shop where Lotta Crabtree, the noted entertainer from Grass Valley, made her debut in 1853. Also of interest, quite close to Rough and Ready, are Smartsville and Browns Valley, two faded gold camps with some stone ruins; these lie just to the west, off Highway 20.

North of Rough and Ready, however, on the Bridgeport Road, is Bridgeport, some 10 miles distant. Its great attraction is its 230-foot covered bridge, built from native timber and with an attractive shingle exterior, believed to be the longest single-span covered bridge in existence in the country. Originally built in 1862, it was in use until 1971, at which time all motor traffic was diverted to the present highway bridge, just to the east. It is now open to the public for walking, and it has some fine views of the Yuba River from its tiny windows. There are some good picnicking places by the river here, quite popular with weekend vacationers.

Farther still, 3 miles, is French Corral, a modest rural center, with an impressive community hall dating from the 1850s. French Corral is also the site of the first long distance telephone in the state, established in 1877, linking the Milton Mining Company's headquarters here, to French Lake, some 58 miles away. The old frame building of the Ridge Telephone Company, itself dating from 1853, from where the telephone connection was actually made, can yet be seen on the main road here.

Two miles from French Corral, the Bridgeport Road sweeps back onto Highway 49, and just to the north of the intersection lies North San Juan, founded in about 1850 by a group of Mexican War veterans, and named for its likeness to a hill of the same name upon which they had fought. There is a brick Wells Fargo Building here, dating from the 1850s, and a cemetery of some historic interest lying just to the west of town.

Nevada City

Immediately north of Grass Valley on Highway 49 is picturesque Nevada City, built on a series of noble hills, and with a unique town plan, where streets radiate out from the center of town, like the spokes in a wheel, following the old, well-worn paths of early miners who panned gold at the ancient Deer Creek Plaza (near the bottom end of present day Broad Street), dispersing in all directions at the end of the day, to their homes. But besides its curious and lovely setting, Nevada City has something else. It is rich in splendid Victorian architecture, perhaps more so than any other town in the Gold Country, filled with elegantly restored homes and fine buildings. It must also be fair to say that this is a town which can only really be seen by walking — although there is a horse-drawn carriage available for hire here as well. In any case, "walking tour" maps of the town can be obtained at the Chamber of Commerce office on Main Street.

One of the most interesting places to visit here is the American Victorian Museum on Spring Street, which has the distinction of being the only museum in the country dedicated exclusively to the collecting, preserving and exhibiting of artifacts from the Victorian Period (1837-1901). There are several very beautiful Victorian objects on display here, including a tracker-action pipe organ built in 1871 by noted pioneer organ builder, Josef Mayer. The museum also has a fine dining room and lounge, but even more importantly, it is itself housed in an historic building of much interest — the old Miners' Foundry — which dates from 1856 and where in 1878 the first Pelton Wheel was cast. Near to the museum, also worth investigating, is the Nevada City Winery, with a good selection of local wines; it is open to the public for tasting, daily 12-2.

Just to the north of the museum on Broad Street one can search out the age-old New York Hotel, rebuilt in 1857 and now housing a half-dozen or so small specialty shops; the red-brick Firehouse No. 2, dating from 1861, and quite photogenic; and the restored Nevada Theatre, originally built in 1865 and said to be the oldest theater building in California still in use. The Foothill Theatre Company now performs here, in spring, summer and fall, with some delightful comedy and drama. Also see the wood-frame United Methodist Church just up the hill from the theater; it dates from 1864. Many other historically interesting buildings can be explored on Broad Street as well, such as the impressive stone and brick I.O.O.F. Hall, and the venerable National Hotel which consists of four adjoining buildings, dating from 1854-1857, and is believed to be the oldest hotel in continuous

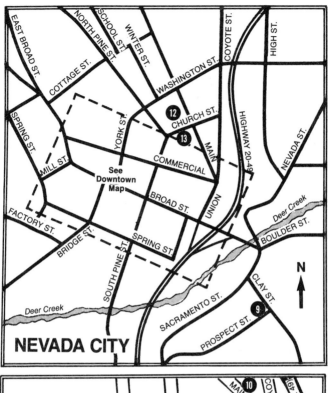

NEVADA CITY

DOWNTOWN

Points of Interest -
1) National Hotel (1854-1857)
2) South Yuba Canal Bldg. (1850s)
3) Ott's Assay Office (1859)
4) Methodist Church
5) Nevada Theatre (1865)
6) Firehouse No. 2 (1861)
7) American Victorian Museum (1856)
8) Nevada City Winery
9) Red Castle (1860)
10) Firehouse No. 1 (1861)
11) New York Hotel (1857)
12) Nevada County Courthouse (1939)
13) Searles Library

operation in the state. Here, too, is to be found the unusual City Hall, dating from 1939 and exhibiting a unique "mid-modern" architectural style, contrasting oddly with the surrounding Victorians; another example of this rather stark architecture is the County Courthouse building on Church Street, some blocks to the north.

A little way from the National Hotel, at the head of Main and Union streets, stands the ancient stone-brick Yuba Canal Building, where in the 1850s one of the state's first major water companies — the forerunner of P.G. & E. (Pacific Gas & Electric), California's giant utility — was established, incorporating several smaller pioneer ditch companies. The building now houses the local Chamber of Commerce, and adjacent to it is the old Ott Assay Office, where in June of 1859 J.J. Ott assayed the first ore samples from the Comstock Lode of Virginia City, Nevada, setting off the great silver rush to the sagebrush state. Close by also is a display of a 5-stamp mill, rescued from Nevada City's Fortuna Mine; it dates from 1893.

Two of Nevada City's most attractive buildings, which you should try to see, are the Red Castle on Prospect Hill, a fine example of Gothic Revival architecture, dating from 1860, which now is a bed and breakfast inn; and the Firehouse No. 1, a charming Victorian with a quaint bell-tower, dating from 1861. The firehouse is now home to the Nevada County Historical Society Museum, where displays are of pioneer 19th century life, predating the mining era, such as relics of the Donner Party and early Chinese artifacts. Take the time also to visit the Trinity Episcopal Church on Nevada street, dating from 1873. It is, most notably, built on the site of Nevada City's very first store, Caldwell's Upper Store, built here in 1849.

Malakoff Diggins and North Bloomfield

Some 15 miles northeast of Nevada City — either on the wild North Bloomfield Road, or on the Tyler-Foote Crossing Road which goes off Highway 49 farther to the north of Nevada City and which has upon it the gold camp of North Columbia, with an 1800s schoolhouse — one arrives at the Malakoff Diggins, the most stunning of all the sights in the Gold Country. Nearly half of a mountain has been torn away here, creating in time a spectacle of unusual beauty: the great expanse of exposed rock rising in magnificent spires and minarets, with colors ranging from sand-white to deep ochre, to rust, and, at times, even a flaming red. This quite notably is also the largest hydraulic gold mine in the world — 7,000 feet long, 3,000 feet wide and 600 feet deep — which operated from 1866 until 1884, washing out some 30 million yards of gravel between 1870 and 1883 alone. In 1884, of course, Judge Lorenzo Sawyer's landmark decision, outlawing the dumping of mine tailings into rivers and streams, effectively ended California's free-spirited hydraulicking era and forced such mines as the Malakoff to close permanently. The "diggins" are now preserved as part of a 2,700-acre state historic park.

There is a lookout on the North Bloomfield Road just above the Malakoff Diggins, which offers superb views of the cut-away mountain and its vast mine-pit. A 3-mile loop trail meanders through the pit for

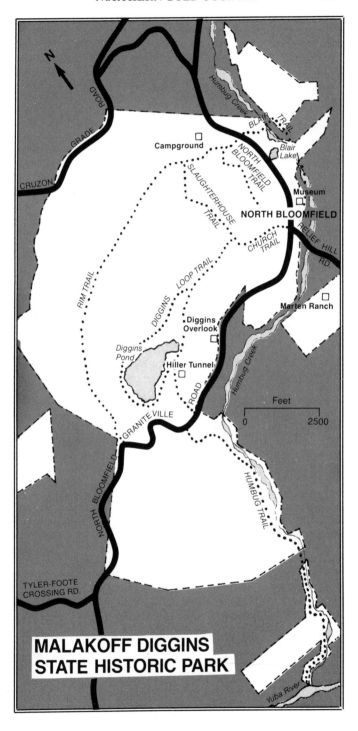

MALAKOFF DIGGINS STATE HISTORIC PARK

closer viewing, and along this one can also see a 556-foot bedrock tunnel, constructed in the 1870s, into which the water and gravels were drained. Another trail leads over the Malakoff rim, quite rewarding scenically. Some other trails, of varying lengths and descriptions, can also be enjoyed here, and just to the east of the Malakoff Ravine, overlooking the "diggins," is a primitive 30-site campground, with a small lake quite close to it, ideal for swimming and fishing.

Also overlooking the Malakoff Diggins is the small but well-preserved town of North Bloomfield, which has a visitor center filled with hydraulic mining memorabilia. In town, too, is displayed one of the hydraulic "monitors" that devoured part of the Malakoff mountain. (A "monitor," incidentally, is an out-size high-pressure nozzle, much like an early-day cannon, invented in 1853 by a Nevada City miner, E.E. Matteson. It was used to direct large quantities of water — under pressure — at mountainsides, which eventually would disintegrate, washing down gold-bearing gravels and rocks into prepared sluices; a typical 9-inch nozzle required some 30,000 gallons of water per minute to operate.)

North Bloomfield also has some historically interesting buildings, dating from the 1870s and 1880s, mainly. The McKillican & Mobley Store, for one, has left on its shelves several pioneer items, dating from the 19th century; and at the Ostrom Livery Stable, there are some delightful exhibits of old wagons. There are a few restored old homes here as well, and just out from the center of town stands the lovely St. Columncille's Catholic Church, originally built in 1860 at Birchville (near French Corral), and re-erected here in 1971. Near to the church are an 1860s schoolhouse and an historic cemetery, both quite interesting to the visitor. Nearby, also, are the sites of one or two smaller hydraulic mines.

East to Washington

Another worthwhile detour from Nevada City is Washington, 13 miles east on Highway 20 and five north off the highway along a pretty side road, descending steeply into the Yuba River — South Fork — canyon. But before Washington, there is Scott's Flat Lake, reached on a small, wild sort of road, south off the highway (20) at the historic Five Mile House (which is now a delightful restaurant). Scott's Flat is a popular recreation lake, completely surrounded by picturesque, wooded hills, and with some beach areas as well as camping, fishing, boating and picnicking possibilities.

Washington itself is a small town, and one of the oldest in the Northern Mines area. Worth seeing here are the old Washington Hotel, with its overhanging balconies; the Kohler Building, dating from 1854 and featuring limestone construction; and the iron-shuttered stone Brimskill Building, built in 1849 and said to be the oldest structure in the county. Some other old, tumbledown buildings can also be seen here and there, and just out from town, along the banks of the Yuba are numerous little piles of rocks — left there by the 49ers, in their back-breaking struggle in the search for gold. This also is great fishing country, with some lovely picnic places.

Also visit the Alpha-Omega Lookout on Highway 20 just east of

Washington, which has good views of the sites of the Alpha and Omega mines which operated here for several years, producing in excess of $1.5 million in gold. The Omega Mine closed in 1949.

THE DOWNIEVILLE AREA

The principal attractions of the Sierra County — the seat of which is Downieville — are its pine forests and rugged granite mountains, and the many outdoor recreation opportunities. This is surely the most scenic area in the Northern Mines, which takes in, besides Downieville, the Sierra Valley, Sierra City, and Alleghany. Two other places included in this area but lying outside Sierra County, are Camptonville and the Plumas-Eureka State Park, the latter exceptionally beautiful.

Camptonville to Downieville

It is roughly 50 miles from Nevada City to Downieville, northeast on Highway 49. But before reaching Downieville there are two places worthy of note. First, there is Camptonville, where in 1878 Lester Pelton invented the famous Pelton Wheel; the town has erected a plaque to commemorate the great event. Also of interest here are an old schoolhouse, an old, wooden jailhouse, and the two-story Mayo Building, dating from 1908.

From Camptonville it is possible to journey 17 miles northeast on Highway 49 to Goodyears Bar — a tiny, shaded village with a few old homes — then follow a wild, mountainous road south 13 miles or so to Alleghany, weaving madly through some unbelievably remote country where heavily forested hills reach deep into equally dense valleys. (An easier way to reach Alleghany is on Ridge Road, which goes off Highway 49 some miles to the south of Camptonville.) Alleghany itself has very little to interest the visitor, except an historic cemetery, but there is much of that wild and beautiful country surrounding the old mining town, especially favored for deer hunting. Alleghany is also the site of the Original Sixteen To One Mine, established in 1896 and named for one of the campaign slogans of William Jennings Bryan, an early-day candidate for President of the United States. The mine produced in excess of $26 million in gold, and closed in 1965.

Back on Highway 49, some 4 miles east of Goodyears Bar is Downieville, the lovliest of all towns in the Northern Mines. It sits astride the rivers Downie and Yuba (North Fork), surrounded by astonishingly beautiful pine-clad mountains, with frame cottages clinging to the mountainsides. Downieville is also steeped in history. The town's main street teems with tales of early miners and their "rich strikes," and it has upon it some very lovely, old buildings — notably, the stone-brick Hirschfelter Building, dating from 1852; the native-stone Mountain Messenger Building, also built in 1852; and the large brick Craycroft Building, again from the same year, and which once was a saloon with one of the longest bars in California — all of 70 feet long. Also, here,

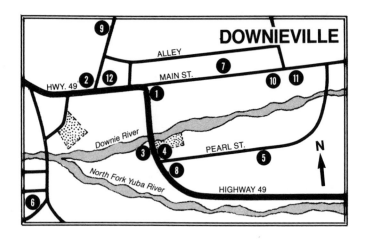

Points of Interest -
1) Craycroft Bldg. (1852)
2) Hirschfeldter Bldg. (1852)
3) I.O.O.F. Hall (1864)
4) Masonic Hall (1864)
5) Old Foundry (1872)
6) Old Gallows

7) Mountain Messenger Bldg. (1852)
8) Methodist Church (1865)
9) Catholic Church (1858)
10) Museum
11) Blacksmith Shop (1896)
12) Bell Tower (1896)

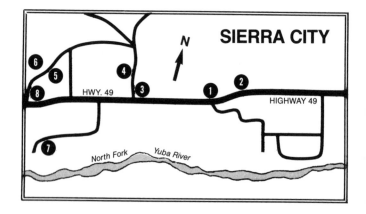

Points of Interest -
1) Busch Building (1871)
2) I.O.O.F. Hall (1870s)
3) Masonic Hall (1863)
4) Methodist Church (1883)

5) Catholic Church (1903)
6) Cemetery (1850s)
7) Sierra Buttes Mine Office Bldg. (1886)
8) Zerloff Hotel (1880s)

one can search out the Masonic and I.O.O.F. Halls, both built in 1864; the old foundry, 1872; the Catholic Church, dating from 1858 and located just above town; and the lovely wood-frame Methodist Episcopal Church, with its quaint tower and huge doors, originally built in 1865 and said to be the oldest Protestant Church in continuous use in California. The local museum on Main Street is worth a visit as well, housed in a most attractive stone building which formerly was a Chinese gambling house, built in 1852; museum displays are of 19th-century relics mostly, and include a miniature stamp mill and a set of old bank gold scales.

At the western end of town is a public park containing many interesting exhibits of early mining equipment, including a Pelton Wheel, arrastra, ore-car, stamp mill, and one or two hydraulic monitors. And a little way to the south of the park, across the river, stands the county courthouse, near to which can also be found the town's original gallows, built in the 1880s, which witnessed a rash of grisly hangings and gave the town much of its early day notoriety. In fact, it was in Downieville in 1851 that one of the most controversial hangings took place, when a Mexican dance-hall girl named Juanita, accused of stabbing an American miner to death, became the first woman ever to be hanged in the Gold Country. The event was all the more dramatic for it was staged on a day of national celebration, Fourth of July, and there was some debate over whether the woman was with child at the time of hanging.

To the east of town, a short walk along the Downie River will lead you to some delightful waterfalls, especially picturesque in spring.

Sierra City and Sierra Valley

The stretch of country between Downieville and Sierra City — some 12 miles — is most rewarding, with the River Yuba rushing alongside of the highway and wildflower-covered canyon walls rolling back into lush, pine forests. Sierra City itself has something of beauty, too; adjoining to its north are the uniquely attractive Sierra Buttes — a mass of stark, rocky mountains, barren of all vegetation, poking up in numerous pinnacles and ledges. At least a dozen different mines operated here between 1850 and the late 1890s, honeycombing the Buttes with hundreds of shafts and tunnels. The Sierra Buttes Mine, best known of all, operated here from the early 1850s until 1937, producing in excess of $17 million in gold.

Sierra City is small, charming, and has many historically interesting buildings, the most notable among which is the clay-brick Busch Building in the center of town, dating from 1871 and erected by the E. Clampus Vitus fraternity which was originally established in Sierra City in 1857. Worth seeing, too, are the 2½-story Zerloff Hotel, with its splendid balconies, dating from the 1880s; the Masonic Hall, 1863; the I.O.O.F. Hall, built in the 1870s; the lovely Methodist Church, with its impressive bell-tower, dating from 1883; and the large Sierra Buttes Mine Office Building, dating from 1886 and now a private residence. This last is actually located just south of the main street, but can be viewed from the highway. Several other age-old homes can also be seen here, though quite at random, and there is a cemetery of some interest at the northwestern end of town, where the oldest graves date from the 1850s.

One of the highlights of Sierra City, that no one should miss, is the Kentucky Mine, now a county park and museum, lying just to the east of town. It has in it one of the only fully operational stamp mills in the country, rebuilt in the 1920s; there are six different levels to it, and here one can actually study the various stages of gold-ore processing. Guided tours of the mill are conducted by park personnel daily in summer. Also, near to the mill one can see the portal of a 1,500-foot horizontal mine shaft, and a working Pelton Wheel. At the museum are more mining artifacts and tools, as well as ore samples, pioneer household items, a schoolhouse exhibit, and pioneer ski exhibits. On the museum grounds outside are other mining displays, such as an iron hoist cage rescued from nearby Monarch Mine, and a typical miner's cabin.

Eastward still, the highway threads the Yuba Pass (6,701 feet), then descends into the delectable Sierra Valley, with its green and purple alfalfa fields sweeping across to the edge of delightfully-wooded mountains; and on the highway here are strung the tiny townships of Sattley, Sierraville, Loyalton, and Vinton — the northern terminus of the Mother Lode Highway. Vinton also has a century-old schoolhouse, and at Loyalton there is a worthwhile museum, with displays of 19th-century relics and antique agricultural and logging equipment.

The Lakes Basin

There remains yet another delightful area to explore. Some miles out from Sierra City, the Gold Lake Road disentangles itself from the highway (49) and climbs north through a rather lovely stretch of country known as the Lakes Basin, which has some 45 different lakes, most of them small, peaceful, and with elevations of over 6,000 feet. These also have good harvests of trout, and camping, picnicking, swimming and hiking. The gorgeous Pacific Crest Trail, with its astounding scenery, passes just to the west of here.

Of all the lakes perhaps Gold and Sardine are of greatest interest to the visitor; both have comfortable guest lodges, originally built in the early 1900s, and it is possible to rent fishing boats at either of the resorts. Sardine Lake has an added attraction: at Upper Sardine, which actually lies to the south of Lower Sardine, we once again find that surprising cluster of mountains, the Sierra Buttes, their majestic mass reflected in the crystal waters of the lake. Gold Lake, on the other hand, has the distinction of being the largest and most important of all the lakes in the area, lying at approximately the center of the Lakes Basin. It also has a mystery about it. It is said that in the winter of 1849, a soldier-miner named Thomas Stoddart accidentally came upon a lake in these parts, the shores of which, he claimed, were laden with gold. But, as the story goes, a group of hostile Indians ambushed and killed his companion, wounding him, and he fled for his life. He returned in the spring, nevertheless, accompanied by scores of eager miners, but never again was he able to find his fairytale "gold lake." The Gold Lake here is then named for Stoddart's mysterious lake,

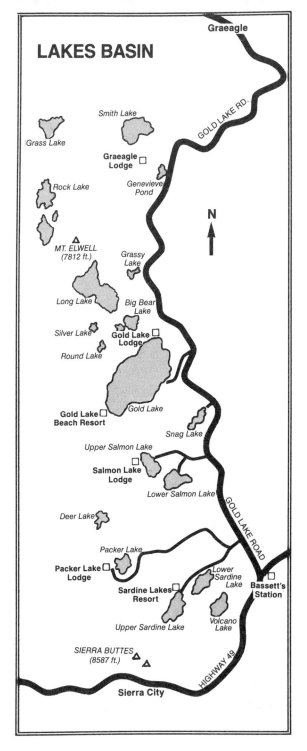

LAKES BASIN

Graeagle

GOLD LAKE RD.

Smith Lake

Grass Lake

Graeagle Lodge

Genevieve Pond

N

Rock Lake

△ MT. ELWELL (7812 ft.)

Grassy Lake

Long Lake

Big Bear Lake

Silver Lake

Gold Lake Lodge

Round Lake

Gold Lake

Gold Lake Beach Resort

Snag Lake

Upper Salmon Lake

Salmon Lake Lodge

Lower Salmon Lake

Deer Lake

Packer Lake

Packer Lake Lodge

Lower Sardine Lake

Bassett's Station

Sardine Lakes Resort

Upper Sardine Lake

Volcano Lake

GOLD LAKE ROAD

SIERRA BUTTES (8587 ft.) △ △

HIGHWAY 49

Sierra City

though its shores may not be paved with gold. Old timers, however, will tell you that there is yet a "gold lake" out there somewhere, the shores of which are indeed paved with gold.

Immediately above the Lakes Basin on Highway 89 (which intersects the Gold Lake Road to the north) is Graeagle, billed as "The Home of the World's Finest Golf Clubs." Here are four exceptional golf courses to enjoy, besides which the town has some good resort areas with tennis and horseback riding, and rafting possibilities on a small, adjoining lake.

Plumas-Eureka State Park

The Plumas-Eureka State Park, 4 miles west of Graeagle on county road A-14, is lapped in scenic luxury. Here are 6,749 acres of stunning woodlands containing great glacier-carved mountains and placid, clear-water lakes, fed by equally lovely snowmelt creeks. It is indeed one of the most scenic mining areas of California, and one of the highest, with elevations ranging between 4,000 feet and 8,000 feet. It also has in it an old mining town, Johnsville, where there are some restored frame homes, mostly privately owned, and a church of some interest, with an ancient bell. The town was originally established in the 1870s by the Sierra Buttes Mining Company, one of the most notable in the area, which operated here from 1867 until 1897.

There is an excellent museum at the park, beautifully kept, and housed in an old miners' boarding house which dates from the 1800s. It has displays of mining artifacts, such as handmade tools, miniature models of a stamp mill and arrastra, and an "assay room" exhibit; also ore samples, nature exhibits, pioneer household items, old photographs, and some superb pioneer ski displays, including the 25-pound wooden skis of "Snowshoe" Thompson, who carried mail through the winter snows, on skis, between Placerville and Genoa, Nevada during the 1850s. On the museum grounds outside are several restored and partially restored buildings of the Plumas-Eureka Mine, including a huge, five-story 60-stamp mill where more than $8 million worth of gold was processed.

The park also has a much-liked campground, popular with summer vacationers, and great fishing and walking opportunities. There is, for instance, a short, easy trail that journeys one-half mile east from the campground to the site of the ancient Jamison Mines, and another, the Eureka Peak Loop Trail, which sets out from the picturesque Eureka Lake to lead to the 7,447-foot Eureka Peak, with good, all-round views from the top; the Eureka Mountain is itself most interesting, honeycombed with over 70 miles of mine workings: it was the scene of much mining activity during the 1870s and 1880s. There are several other quite rewarding trails here as well, and the park association also publishes a "jogger's map."

Another place of interest at the park is the pioneer ski area just above Johnsville — reached on a steep park road, about a mile — where ski races were first held in 1861, and which has in it one of the world's oldest ski lifts. Now the Plumas-Eureka Ski Bowl, the ski area is operated by the Plumas County Ski Club and is open to the public on weekends in winter.

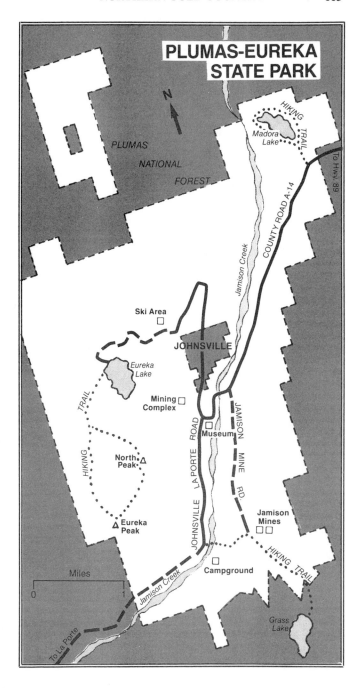

PLUMAS-EUREKA
STATE PARK

N

PLUMAS

NATIONAL

FOREST

Jamison Creek

COUNTY ROAD A-14

To Hwy 89

HIKING TRAIL

Madora Lake

Ski Area

JOHNSVILLE

Eureka Lake

Mining Complex

TRAIL

HIKING

North Peak

Eureka Peak

JOHNSVILLE LA PORTE ROAD

Museum

JAMISON MINE RD.

Jamison Mines

HIKING TRAIL

Miles

0

Jamison Creek

Campground

To La Porte

Grass Lake

PRACTICAL INFORMATION FOR NORTHERN GOLD COUNTRY

 HOW TO GET THERE. All major towns in the Northern Gold Country — Auburn, Grass Valley, Nevada City and Downieville — are conveniently located on *Highway 49* (the Mother Lode Highway) which runs from Vinton in the north to Oakhurst in the south, a length of 316 miles, with roughly 130 miles of it passing through the Northern Gold Country. In addition, there are some good east-west highways linking Auburn, Grass Valley and Nevada City to other important towns of Northern California.

The following are some of the recommended routes to the main towns of the area.

Auburn. The most direct and best way to reach Auburn is on *Interstate 80*, either from San Francisco and Sacramento or from Reno, Nevada in the east. Auburn is 20 miles distant from Sacramento, and approximately 120 miles from San Francisco.

Grass Valley-Nevada City. These twin townships are linked from the west and east by *Highway 20*. It is approximately 35 miles from Marysville and Yuba City in the west to Grass Valley, and another 4 miles north on *Highway 49* to Nevada City. Alternatively, you can travel to Auburn on *Interstate 80*, then go north on *Highway 49*, some 25 miles, to Grass Valley.

Downieville is 50 miles northeast of Grass Valley on *Highway 49*.

 HOTELS AND RESTAURANTS. All major towns in the Northern Gold Country — such as Auburn, Grass Valley and Nevada City — have comfortable accommodations and good dining facilities. These include historic hostelries and quaint bed and breakfast inns, in addition to motels. But expect hotel rates to be slightly higher on weekends and holidays, and during the peak, summer season it is advisable to book ahead. Reservations in the Auburn area can be made through the *Auburn Area Visitors & Convention Bureau* by calling, toll free, (800) 433-7575; in the Grass Valley-Nevada City area call the *Nevada County Chamber of Commerce* — (800) 752-6222 in California, or (800) 521-2075 from out of state.

Rates for accommodations, based on double occupancy, are categorized as follows: *Deluxe* (D), over $65; *Expensive* (E), $55-$65; *Moderate* (M), $40-$55; *Inexpensive* (I), under $40. (Note: rates are subject to change, and a sales tax will be added to your motel bill.)

Restaurant prices — based on a full course meal, excluding drinks, tax and tips — are categorized as follows: *Deluxe* (D), over $25; *Expensive* (E), $15-$25; *Moderate* (M), $10-$15; *Inexpensive* (I), under $10.

Most hotels and restaurants in the area accept major credit cards, but it is always worth inquiring beforehand.

AUBURN. Bed & Breakfast. *Power's Mansion Inn* (D), 164 Cleveland Ave., (916) 885-1166; 15 lavishly decorated rooms in century-old Victorian mansion; also bridal suite with fireplace and sunken heart-shaped tub. Complimentary wine and epicurean breakfast. *Lincoln House Inn* (M-E), 191 Lincoln Way, (916) 885-8880; small restored cottage with great mountain views; 3 rooms. Complimentary drinks, homemade breakfast with pastries, breads, fresh fruit and juice. *The Victorian* (E-D), P.O. Box 9097, Auburn 95603, (916) 885-5879; 1850s Victorian home set on seven splendid acres overlooking Auburn; garden, gazebo, hot tub and sauna. 3 rooms, 2 with baths. *Dry Creek Inn* (E-D), 13740 Dry Creek Road, (916) 878-0885; creekside setting, one bedroom with bath and study, and one suite. Reservations only. *Old Auburn Inn* (M), 149 Pleasant Ave., (916) 885-6407; country inn with 2 lovely rooms; breakfast in dining room.

Motels. *Foothills Motel* (I), I-80 at Foresthill exit, (916) 885-8444; 62 rooms, TV, phones, free coffee, pool and spa. *Auburn Inn* (M), 1875 Auburn Ravine Rd., (916) 885-1800. 85 rooms, TV, pool, spa, senior citizen discounts. *Golden Key Motel* (M), 13450 Lincoln Way, (916) 885-8611; 50 units, TV, phones, pool, AAA. *Elmwood Motel* (I), 588 High St., (916) 885-5186; 24 rooms, TV, phones, pool. *Country Squire Inn* (I-M), 13480 Lincoln Way, (916) 885-7025; 80 units, TV, phones, restaurant.

Restaurants. *Butterworths* (E), cnr. Lincoln Way and Court St., (916) 885-0249; superb gourmet cuisine, served in Victorian setting. Open 11.30-9, dinners and lunch; also Sunday brunch. *Gold Rush Plaza Restaurant* (M), 111 Sacramento St., (916) 888-6448; homemade soups and biscuits, also seafood and steaks. *North Fork Dry Diggins* (M-E), cnr. Bell Rd. and Hwy. 49, (916) 885-4762; continental and American fare, Sunday Champagne Brunch, dancing. Open Mon.-Sat., lunch and dinner. *Headquarter House* (E), 14500 Musso Rd. (just east of Auburn), (916) 878-1906; traditional American fare, with steak specialties; splendid country setting. Open for lunch and dinner daily, brunch on Sundays; reservations recommended. *The Grand Old Auburn Hotel* (M-E), 853 Lincoln Way, (916) 885-8132; Basque family dinners daily; also breakfast, lunch and Sunday brunch. Piano bar.

GRASS VALLEY. **Bed & Breakfast.** *Annie Horan's* (E-D), 415 W. Main St., (916) 272-2418; 1874 Victorian with 4 antique furnished rooms. Breakfast patio and spacious deck. *Domike's Inn* (M-D), 220 Colfax Ave., (916) 273-9010; restored Queen Anne with 4 delightful rooms. Complimentary wine and snacks, wholesome breakfast. *Golden Ore House* (E-D), 448 S. Auburn St., (916) 272-6870; charming turn-of-the-century home in wooded setting; 6 rooms with Victorian decor. Breakfast served on deck. No smokers, no pets. *Murphys Inn* (E-D), 318 Neal St., (916) 273-6873; 3 enchanting rooms filled with antiques, in former home of gold baron Edward Coleman, owner of North Star and Idaho-Maryland mines; home dates from 1866. Complimentary wine and sherry, country club privileges. *Swan-Levine House* (M-E), 328 S. Church St., (916) 272-1873; turreted 3-story Victorian, built in 1880; 4 artistically decorated rooms, one with bath. Studio space, art instruction.

Hotels and Motels. *Holbrooke Hotel* (M-D), 212 W. Main St., (916) 273-1353; historic 1851 hostelry; 28 restored guest rooms with antique furnishings. Restaurant on premises. *Holiday Lodge* (M), 1221 E. Main St., (916) 273-4406; 36 units, TV, phones, pool, sauna, hot tub; also ask about their holiday package, with gold panning and historical highlight tour. *Gold Country Inn* (M), 11972 Sutton Way, (916) 273-1393; 84 rooms, TV, phones, pool, spa. *Golden Chain Resort Motel* (M), 13363 Hwy. 49, (916) 273-7279; 21 units, TV, phones, pool, picnic area. *Mitchell's Motel* (I-M), 12390 Hwy. 20, (916) 273-8433; 10 units, TV, pool, lawns. *Alta Sierra Motel* (M-D), 135 Tammy Way, (916) 273-9102; 11 units, TV, country club. *Coach & Four Motel* (I-M), 628 S. Auburn St., (916) 273-8009; 16 units, TV, continental breakfast.

Restaurants. *Dragon Seed Inn* (M), cnr. Colfax Hwy. and Brunswick

Rd., (916) 273-0520; established Chinese restaurant serving Cantonese and Szechwan dishes. Open Wed.-Sun. *Sutter's Mill* (M-E), 13480 Hwy. 49 (just south of Grass Valley), (916) 273-0388; prime rib specialty; also chicken, seafood, tempura, and fettucini. Deck available for outdoor dining; attractively priced Sunday brunch. Open for lunch and dinner. *Scheidel's* (M-E), on Alta Sierra Dr. (off Hwy. 49), (916) 273-5553; traditional European cooking. Open Wed.-Sun. *Marshall's Pasties* (I-M), 203 Mill St. (916) 272-2844; splendid variety of freshly-baked Cornish pasties and English sausage rolls. *The Owl Tavern* (M-E), 134 Mill St. (916) 273-0526; homemade Cornish pasties, prime rib, lobster; old "English Pub" atmosphere. Lunch and dinner daily; reservations recommended.

NEVADA CITY. Bed & Breakfast. *Flume's End* (D), 317 South Pine St., (916) 265-9665; restored Victorian with terraces opening onto waterfall; 3 rooms and charming honeymoon cottage. Hearty breakfast, evening cocktails. *Red Castle Inn* (E-D), 109 Prospect Ave., (916) 265-5135; 4-story picture-book Victorian Gothic mansion, circa 1860; overlooking Nevada City. 8 lovely rooms, porches and gardens; continental breakfast. No children or pets. *Piety Hill Inn* (M-E), 523 Sacramento St., (916) 265-2245; individual cottages with sitting room and breakfast area; antique furnishings.

Hotels and Motels. *National Hotel* (M-D), 211 Broad St., (916) 265-4551; historic 1850s hotel, oldest in California in continuous use. 43 guest rooms, Victorian furnishings; dining room, cocktail lounge, pool. *Northern Queen Motel* (I-M), 400 Railroad Ave., (916) 265-5824; 40 rooms, TV, phones, in-room coffee, pool, jacuzzi; also has individual cottages. *Rancho Motel* (I-M), 760 Zion St., (916) 265-2253; 20 rooms, TV, pool, kitchenettes. *Airway Motel* (I), 575 E. Broad St. (916) 265-2233; 12 rooms, TV, pool.

Restaurants. *National Hotel* (M-E), 211 Broad St., (916) 265-4551; American and Continental dishes, served in Victorian dining room. Lunch and dinner daily; reservations suggested. Jack's (D), 101 Sacramento St., (916) 265-3405; fine international cuisine, 5-course dinners. Menu changes daily. Reservations required. *Friar Tuck's* (M-E), 111 N. Pine St., (916) 265-9093; Swiss and French fondue dinners; also steaks and seafood. Reservations recommended; closed Mon. *Selaya's* (E-D), 320 Broad St., (916) 265-5697; California cuisine and fresh seafood specialties. Dinners from 6 p.m., Tues.-Sun. Reservations required. *Michael's Garden Restaurant* (E-D), 216 Main St., (916) 265-6660; creative seafood; favorites are hot and spicy prawns, baked duckling, chicken in filo. Reservations required.

DOWNIEVILLE. *Downieville Motor Inn* (I-M), Hwy. 49, (916) 289-3243; 12 units, TV, kitchenettes.

Restaurant. *Quartz Cafe* (I-M), Main St., (916) 289-3241; casual eatery, serving hamburgers, soups and chili. Open for breakfast and lunch.

GRAEAGLE. *Gray Eagle Lodge* (D), off Gold Lake Rd. (just south of Graeagle), (916) 836-2511; 15 vacation cabins in wooded, creekside setting; meals included. Reservations.

 TOURIST INFORMATION. Visitor information is quite readily available in the Northern Gold Country, at local chambers of commerce, museums and state park offices. However, if you are traveling extensively in the gold region, a complete Gold Country map is much to be recommended: the Golden Chain Council publishes *The Mother Lode Highway Map* which also contains points of interest in the various counties, and Compass Maps' *Gold Map* is quite good, too. Additionally, Nevada and Placer counties publish their own detailed maps.

Chambers of Commerce. *Auburn Area Chamber of Commerce,* 1101 High St., Auburn 95603; (916) 885-5616. Old Town and county maps, plus tourist interest brochures and area services directory. Also, *Colfax Area Chamber of Commerce,* Canyon Way (P.O. Box 86), Colfax 95713; (916) 346-8888. Area map for Colfax, Dutch Flat, Iowa Hill and Gold Run; and tourist literature.

Nevada County/Grass Valley Area Chamber of Commerce, 248 Mill St., Grass Valley 95945; (916) 273-4667. Maps, calendar of events, listings for lodging, dining and recreational facilities; also "walking tour" maps with points of interest.

Nevada County Chamber of Commerce, 132 Main St., Nevada City 95959; (916) 265-2692. "Walking tour" maps of Nevada City downtown, and local interest books; also calendar of events, lodging and restaurant listings, and literature on local winery and the American Victorian Museum.

Sierra County Tourist Commission Information Center, Main St., Downieville 95936; (916) 289-3122. Maps of Downieville, Sierra City and other county towns; also general tourist information.

LOCAL TRANSPORTATION. In **Nevada City-Grass Valley**. The *Gold Country Stage* services both Nevada City and Grass Valley, linking the two towns as well. Fare is 75¢ per trip, or $1.50 for a daily pass; there is a monthly pass available too. For more information, and schedule, call (916) 265-1411.

In the **Auburn Area**. The city of Auburn is serviced by *Placer County Transit*; for a schedule and information, call (916) 885-BUSS.

SEASONAL EVENTS. There are dozens of events held every year in each of the three areas covered in the Northern Gold Country section, and the county chambers of commerce each publish a *Calendar of Events.* The following, however, are some of the long-established events of the area:

FEBRUARY. *Northern Mines Wine Tasting Exposition and Auction,* Grass Valley; California wines, arts and crafts and other displays. Usually held during the last weekend of the month.

APRIL. Second Weekend. *International Teddy Bear Convention,* Nevada City; features teddy bear contests, with entries from all over the world; also some historical displays, and vendor stalls.

Third Weekend. *Annual House and Garden Tour,* Nevada City; see *Tours* section.

Fourth Weekend. *Penn Valley Rodeo,* Penn Valley (8 miles east of Grass Valley); among the largest rodeos in the state, includes pit barbeque.

JUNE. First Weekend. *Miners' Picnic,* Empire Mine State Park, Grass Valley; features traditional Cornish miners' picnic, food stalls, mucking contest, gold panning. *Gold Country Marathon,* Nevada City; full marathon and 10,000-meter races.

Second Weekend. *Malakoff Homecoming,* North Bloomfield (Nevada City area); parade, local interest movies, square dancing, children's games, and other celebrations.

Third Weekend. *Nevada City Classic,* Nevada City; one of America's most prestigious bicycle races, with top amateur and professional cyclists competing. *Summer Bluegrass Festival,* Grass Valley; bluegrass groups perform. *Music in the Mountains,* Grass Valley and Nevada City; 16 days of festivals and concerts, some workshops.

Fourth Weekend. *Folsom Championship Rodeo,* Folsom (17 miles south of Auburn); largest Fourth-of-July rodeo in the country. *Rough and Ready Secession Days Celebration,* Rough and Ready (5 miles east of Grass Valley); continuous, all-day entertainment, chuckwagon breakfast. *Sierra Festival of the Arts,* Grass Valley; arts and crafts displays, including children's art, and food stalls and entertainment.

JULY. *July 4th Celebration,* Grass Valley; parade, a variety of games and entertainment, and refreshments. Third Weekend. *Gold Country Panning Championship and Gold Fair,* Auburn; panning contests, mining equipment sales and demonstrations, live country western music, Old West shootouts.

AUGUST. *Nevada County Fair,* Grass Valley; concerts, rodeos, destruction derby, loggers' olympics, and other festivities; also some exhibits. Held on last weekend of month.

SEPTEMBER. Second Weekend. *Gold Country Fair,* Auburn; musical entertainment, horse show, rodeo, four-wheel-drive-pulls, motorcycle racing, and exhibits.

OCTOBER. First Weekend. *Oktoberfest,* Grass Valley; Bavarian food, music and dancing, and other entertainment.

NOVEMBER. First Weekend. *Annual Gold Country Quilt Show,* Nevada City; a wearable art fashion show, and historic quilts display.

Third and Fourth Weekends. *Cornish Christmas,* Grass Valley; Cornish treats, Santa Claus, music and entertainment.

DECEMBER. *Cornish Christmas,* at Grass Valley (same as above, in November) on first, second and third weekends of the month.

HISTORIC HOME TOURS. *Annual House and Garden Tour,* Nevada City. Tours of selected Victorian homes and historic gardens of Nevada City. Tours are usually conducted on two successive weekends in late April or early May; tour cost is around $7.00 per person. For more information, contact the American Victorian Museum, 325 Spring St., Nevada City 95959; (916) 265-5804.

MINE TOURS. *Empire Mine,* 10787 E. Empire St., Grass Valley; (916) 273-8522. Tour 784-acre mine estate (now part of a state historic park), with its vast surface works, such as headframes, mine buildings, old mining equipment, and, best of all, the picturesque Bourne Cottage — an 1890 Willis Polk-designed stone mansion, former summer residence of William Bourne, Jr. — set on splendid grounds. Also view the main mine shaft, illuminated for some 150 feet. (The Empire, incidentally, was the largest, deepest and richest hardrock gold mine in California: it boasted some 360 miles of underground mine workings, with an inclined depth of over 11,000 feet, and produced an estimated $70 million in gold.) Picture-slide programs included on tour. Guided tours at 1.30 and 3 p.m. daily in summer, and on weekends in spring and fall. Park fee: $1.00 adults, 50¢ children.

Kentucky Mine, Hwy. 49, Sierra City; (916) 862-1310. Guided tours of mine's six-story 10-stamp mill — believed to be the only fully-operational stamp mill in the country. Also view mine portal and see working Pelton Wheel. Museum on premises. Tours conducted May-Sept., 10-5 Wed.-Sun. Tour cost: $1.50 adults.

Malakoff Diggins, North Bloomfield Star Rt. (13 miles northeast of Nevada City), Nevada City; (916) 265-2740. Visit world's largest hydraulic gold mine — 7,000 feet long, 3,000 feet wide and 600 feet deep. It is possible to walk around the vast mine pit and explore an 1870s drainage tunnel. Also visit interpretive center, with exhibits centered around hydraulic mining. The "diggins" are now part of a state historic park; open 9-4.30 daily.

Plumas-Eureka Mine; located in the Plumas-Eureka State Park (4 miles from Graeagle, west off Hwy. 89 north); (916) 863-2380. Explore mine buildings, old mining equipment, and a partially-restored 60-stamp mill, five stories high, where more than $8 million worth of gold was crushed. Park is open in spring, summer and fall, 8 a.m. until sunset.

WALKING TOURS. *Nevada City* and *Old Town, Auburn* are two of the finest places to explore on foot. "Walking tours" maps of the Nevada City downtown can be obtained at the town's Chamber of Commerce, and Auburn Old Town maps are available at most local merchants, as well as at the local Chamber of Commerce. Also, *Grass Valley* has a small downtown section with beautiful old homes and buildings, quite rewarding to walkers.

Farther north, *North Bloomfield, Downieville* and *Sierra City* are ideally suited to being seen by walking around. Maps of Downieville and Sierra City, with points of interest, are available at the county Chamber of Commerce or the information booth on Main Street in Downieville.

MUSEUMS. *Placer County Museum,* 1273 High St., Auburn (located at the County Fairgrounds). Displays of Indian and Chinese artifacts, some prehistoric items; also relics of the gold rush era and mining displays. Open 10-4, Tues.-Sun. Admission fee: $1.00 adults, 50¢ children; includes tour of adjoining Barnhard House (and winery) — an 1874 stone structure. Museum phone, (916) 885-9570.

North Star Mining Museum, 10933 Allison Ranch Rd., Grass Valley. Housed in 1895 stone building, formerly North Star Mine power-house. Excellent mining displays, including handcrafted tools, Cornish Pump, 20-stamp mill, and 30-foot Pelton Wheel — largest in the world. Some old mining literature for sale. Open 10-5 daily, May-Sept.; admission 50¢. (916) 273-4255.

Grass Valley Museum; housed in old St. Mary's Convent Building at the corner of Church and Chapel Sts., Grass Valley. Museum building dates from 1865. Exhibits of 19th-century classroom, parlor, music room, and doctor's office. Open June-Oct., weekdays 12-3. Phone (916) 272-8188.

Empire Mine State Historic Park, 10791 Empire St., Grass Valley. Interpretive center located at park headquarters; contains some mining tools, old photographs, and recount of history of Empire Mine. Several interesting displays of mining equipment on grounds outside. Open 9-5 daily; park fee: $1.00 adults, 50¢ children. Phone (916) 273-8522.

American Victorian Museum, 328 Spring St., Nevada City. Housed in ancient Miners' Foundry, originally built in 1856. Rotating displays of Victorian artifacts, which include a tracker-action pipe organ built in 1871 by noted pioneer organ builder, Josef Mayer. Hours: 10.30-4, Thurs.-Mon.; donations accepted. (916) 265-5804.

Firehouse #1 Museum, 214 Main St., Nevada City. Relics of Donner Party, early Chinese artifacts, including Joss House, and a fine collection of Maidu Indian baskets. Museum housed in picturesque Victorian building, dating from 1861. Open 11-4 Mon.-Fri. (916) 265-5468.

Malakoff Diggins State Historic Park, North Bloomfield Rd., North Bloomfield. Small museum in park headquarters building; displays of 1800s hydraulic mining memorabilia, including a 9-inch "monitor." Open 10-5 in summer, 9.30-4 on weekends the rest of the year; park fee is $3.00. Phone (916) 265-2740.

Downieville Museum, Main St., Downieville. Housed in 1852 stone building, formerly a Chinese gambling house. Museum displays are of 19th-century relics, such as pioneer clothing, old letters and diaries, photographs, guns, a miniature stamp mill and a set of ancient bank gold scales. Hours: 10-5, May-Sept. No admission fee; donations accepted.

Kentucky Mine Museum; located just off Hwy. 49, 1 mile east of Sierra City. Displays of mining artifacts and tools, ore samples, pioneer household items, a schoolhouse exhibit, and pioneer ski exhibits. On the grounds outside are other interesting exhibits, including an iron hoist cage from a mine, a miner's cabin, a restored 10-stamp mill, and mine portal. Open 10-5, Wed.-Sun., May-Sept.; admission fee: 50¢. (916) 862-1310.

Sierra Valley Museum; located at the Loyalton City Park, Loyalton. Displays centered around local history, featuring agricultural and logging exhibits.

Plumas-Eureka State Park Museum; housed in 1800s miners' boarding house located in the park, on county road A-14 (off Hwy. 89, 4 miles west of Graeagle). Museum displays are of mining artifacts, such as handmade tools, miniature models of a stamp mill and arrastra, and an "assay room" exhibit; also ore samples, nature exhibits, pioneer household items, old photographs, and pioneer ski displays which include the original 25-pound wooden skis of the legendary "Snowshoe" Thompson. Open summers, 10-4; donations accepted. Park phone (916) 836-2380.

HISTORICAL LIBRARIES. *Pacific Library,* cnr. Church and Chapel Sts., Grass Valley (housed in St. Mary's Convent Building). Fine collection of old scientific, reference and history books; some 10,000 books dating from early 16th century to present day. Open June-Oct., weekdays 12-3. (916) 272-8188.

Nevada County Historical Library, 214 Church St., Nevada City. Old books, manuscripts and photographs pertaining to early history of Nevada County. Open Mon.-Sat., 1-4. (916) 265-5910.

 RECREATION LAKES. *Rollins Lake.* Situated just off Hwy. 174, about 11 miles southeast of Grass Valley, the lake has over 900 acres of water, 26 miles of shoreline, and has a maximum depth of 205 feet. Facilities here include camping, fishing, boating, water-skiing, swimming and picnicking. There is also a fully-stocked marina here, with boat rentals, as well as 4 stores and 3 restaurants. Day use fee: $3.50; boat launching $3.50. For information call (916) 346-6166/272-3500

Scotts Flat Lake, on Scotts Flat Rd. (off Hwy. 20), 7 miles east of Nevada City. The lake contains 740 acres of water, approximately 8 miles of shoreline, with an average depth of 180 feet. Facilities include camping, fishing, swimming, picnicking, boat rentals, store, and bait and tackle shop. Day use fee: $3.50; boat launching $3.25. For information call (916) 265-5302.

Also, the *Lakes Basin*, located above Sierra City in the Gold Lake Road (which goes off Hwy. 49), has some small, worthwhile recreation lakes, most with camping, picnicking and swimming, and some with boating. *Gold Lake* and *Sardine Lake* are the two most notable; both have good lodges and boat rentals.

RAFTING. See *Southern Gold Country* section.

FISHING. There is an abundance of good fishing lakes, creeks and rivers in the Northern Gold Country, mainly in the Tahoe National Forest which comprises 813,181 acres and boasts over 350 species of fish. Most commonly found are Rainbow, German, Mackinaw and brown trout, and Kokanee Salmon. The South Yuba River, near Washington, is quite popular with weekend anglers; also the many small lakes in the Lakes Basin area provide some good fishing opportunities.

Fishing licenses can be obtained at one of the Fish and Game Department offices, or from some of the local bait and tackle shops; license fee is around $19.00 for California residents, and there is usually a catch limit of 10 fish.

HUNTING. Wildlife is abundant in the Northern Gold Country, with game birds and deer and bob cats being the most common. The Alleghany area is especially noted for its excellent deer hunting; the season begins in Oct.-Nov.

Hunting licenses are around $18.50 for California residents, with additional amounts for the various tags. For rules, regulations, game limits, and hunting licenses, contact your nearest Fish and Game Department office.

HIKING. The best places for hiking in the Northern Gold Country are the state parks, with nearly 30 miles of some of the most rewarding trails. At the *Plumas-Eureka State Park,* the walker encounters fabulous high-country scenery, with trails circling serene, fresh-water lakes and journeying through splendid pine woods and along enchanting snowmelt creeks. The *Malakoff Diggins State Historic Park* on the other hand has some uniquely picturesque trails, with views of its great hydraulic gold mine: there is even a trail that passes through the mine pit, with opportunities to explore an 1870s drainage tunnel.

Also, in the Lakes Basin, north of Sierra City, there are some worthwhile hiking areas.

GOLF COURSES. *Alta Sierra Golf & Country Club*, 144 Tammy Way, Grass Valley; (916) 273-2010. 18-hole championship course, with driving range, lessons, pro shop, carts; also restaurant and lounge.

Angus Hills Golf Course, 14520 Musso Rd., Auburn; (916) 878-7818. 9-hole, 27-par course; pro shop, driving cage, lessons, snack bar.

Black Oak Golf Course, 2500 Black Rd., Auburn; (916) 878-1900. 9-hole, 36-par course. Pro shop, driving range, lessons. Open year-round.

Nevada County Country Club, 1040 E. Main St., Grass Valley; (916) 273-6436. 9-hole course; pro shop. Open year-round.

Feather River Inn Golf Course, Hwy. 70, Blairsden (just north of Graeagle); (916) 836-2722. 9-hole, 34-par course; lessons.

Graeagle Meadows Golf Course, Graeagle; (916) 836-2323/836-2348. 18-hole championship course; facilities include a driving range, pro shop, lessons, electric carts, and restaurant.

Plumas Pines Golf Club, on county road A-14 (3 miles west off Hwy. 89), Graeagle; (916) 836-1420. 18-hole championship course; pro shop, carts, dining room and lounge.

HORSEBACK RIDING. *Shadow Glen Riding Stables*, 4854 Main St., Fair Oaks (southwest of Auburn); (916) 989-1826. Scenic trail rides, lakeshore riding, lessons, moonlight and day rides. Group rates available.

Lakehills Equestrian Park, 6525 Boulder Rd., Loomis (9 miles southwest of Auburn); (916) 652-4918. Trail rides at nearby Folsom Lake; also lessons.

SKIING. There are several fine ski areas to be found some 45 or 50 miles east of Nevada City (or northeast of Auburn), off I-80.

Downhill Ski Areas. *Boreal Ridge.* 10 miles west of Truckee, just off I-80 (take Castle Peak exit). Elevations: top 7,800 feet, base 7,200 feet; vertical drop 600 feet. Facilities: 9 lifts, night skiing, lessons, rentals, snack bar and restaurant.

Donner Ski Ranch. West of Truckee; take Soda Springs exit off I-80, then 3½ miles down old Highway 40. Elevations: top 7,960 feet, base 7,135 feet; vertical drop 825 feet. Facilities: 6 lifts, night skiing, lessons, rentals, snack bar and restaurant.

Soda Springs. West of Truckee; on old Highway 40, near Soda Springs exit off I-80. Elevations: top 7,352 feet, base 6,700 feet; vertical drop 652 feet. Facilities: 3 lifts, night skiing, snowboarding, lessons and rentals.

Sugar Bowl. West of Truckee; take Soda Springs exit off I-80, then onto old Highway 40. Elevations: top 8,383 feet, base 6,881 feet; vertical drop 1,502 feet. Facilities: 10 lifts and 1 gondola, night skiing, lessons, rentals, snack bar and restaurant.

Tahoe Donner. 2½ miles northwest of Truckee, off Donner Pass Road. Elevations: top 7,350 feet, base 6,750 feet; vertical drop 600 feet. Facilities: 3 lifts, lessons, rentals, snack bar and restaurant.

Nordic Ski Areas. *Royal Gorge.* A mile from I-80, at the Soda Springs exit. 153 miles of trails; tours, restaurant. Phone (916) 426-3871

Tahoe Donner Nordic Center. West of Truckee, ½ mile from I-80, off old Highway 40, 30 miles of trails; tours, lodge. Phone (916) 587-9821.

CAMPGROUNDS AND RV PARKS. There are some good campgrounds in the Northern Gold Country, with facilities ranging from the basic restrooms, showers and piped drinking water, to RV hookups, boating, swimming, fishing, hiking and horseback riding.

In the **Auburn Area.** *Auburn KOA*, 3550 KOA Way (off Hwy. 49, north of Bell Rd.), Auburn; (916) 885-0990. 26 RV spaces with full hookups, water-sewer-electric; 24 pull-through spaces, with RV length not to exceed 35 feet. Also 15 campsites, showers, laundry, store, recreation room, playground, swimming pool, fishing and gold panning. Open year-round. Camping fee: $13.00-$18.00.

Bear River RV and Campground, 6850 Grass Valley Hwy. (8 miles north of Auburn), Auburn; (916) 269-1121. RV spaces with full hookups, pull-through spaces, campsites, dump station, laundry, hot showers, swimming pool, playground, store and gift shop; also, gold panning and fishing in adjoining Bear River. Camping fee: $13.50-$16.50.

In the **Nevada City-Grass Valley Area.** *Rollins Lake,* off Hwy. 174 (11 miles southeast of Grass Valley), Grass Valley; (916) 272-6100. Campsites, marina with boat rentals, stores, restaurants, swimming and fishing, water-skiing, and picnicking. Camping, $10.00-$13.00 per site per night; boat launching, $3.50.

Scott's Flat Lake, 23333 Scotts Flat Rd. (7 miles east of Nevada City), Nevada City; (916) 265-5302. RV spaces, campsites, hot showers, beach, dump station, store, bait and tackle shop, full-service marina with boat rentals. Camping fee: $10.00 per site per night.

River Rest Campground, Washington; (916) 265-4306. RV spaces with full hookups, campsites, group camping area, store, laundry, swimming, hiking, fishing and gold panning. Camping Fee: $10.00-$15.00.

Gene's Pineaire Campground, Washington; (916) 265-2832. RVs and campsites, nearby fishing and gold panning. Camping Fee: $10.00.

Malakoff Diggins State Historic Park, 23579 North Bloomfield-Graniteville Rd., (13 miles northeast of Nevada City), Nevada City; (916) 265-2740. 30 primitive campsites (no hookups or showers), restrooms, drinking water, fishing, swimming and hiking; also, 2 rental cabins for family use, and 50-camper group sites. Trailer length not to exceed 30 feet; campers up to 24 feet. Camping fee: $10.00 per site, per night; rental cabins $15.00 per night.

In the **Downieville Area.** *Sierra Skies RV Park,* Hwy. 49, Sierra City; (916) 862-1166. RV spaces with full hookups, hot showers. Fishing and gold panning in Yuba.

Plumas-Eureka State Park, 4 miles from Graeagle (west off Hwy. 89 north); (916) 836-2380. 67 developed campsites (maximum trailer length 24 feet, campers 30 feet), restrooms, hot showers, laundry tubs, and fishing and hiking. Camping fee: $10.00. Closed in winter.

In addition to the above, there are numerous campgrounds in the Tahoe National Forest — near Washington, Camptonville, Downieville, Foresthill (northeast of Auburn), and the Lakes Basin (directly above Sierra City). Most of these are quite primitive; some are available at no charge, some for a nominal fee of around $6.00, and a day-limit usually applies. For more information on these campgrounds, contact any of the following Forest Service offices: *Downieville Ranger District,* Star Rt. Box 1, Camptonville 95922, (916) 288-3231; *Foresthill Ranger District,* 22830 Foresthill Rd., Foresthill 95631, (916) 367-2224; *Nevada City Ranger District,* 12012 Sutton Way, Grass Valley 95945, (916) 273-1371; *Tahoe National Forest Headquarters,* Hwy. 49 and Coyote St., Nevada City 95959, (916) 265-4531.

STATE HISTORIC PARKS. Empire Mine State Historic Park, E. Empire St., Grass Valley. 749-acre park, established in 1975, consisting of the *Empire Mine* — the largest, deepest and richest hardrock gold mine in California, with nearly 360 miles of underground mine workings. The mine's surface works, which can be toured here, include headframes, mine buildings, and old mining equipment. Also see the lovely *Bourne Cottage* — an 1890 stone home designed by San Francisco's Willis Polk. There is a small interpretive center at the park, with an excellent recount of the history of the Empire Mine. The park also has beautiful grounds, and picnicking possibilities. Park hours: 9-5; park fee: $1.00 adults, 50¢ children. For more information call the park's office on (916) 273-8522.

Malakoff Diggins State Historic Park, North Bloomfield-Graniteville Rd., 13 miles northeast of Nevada City. 2,700-acre park containing the world's largest hydraulic gold mine; elevations of park vary between 2,200 feet and 4,200 feet. Also in the park is the small, neatly restored mining town of *North Bloomfield*, with a museum, mining displays, an ancient church and schoolhouse, and a pioneer cemetery. Camping, hiking, fishing, swimming, picnicking, and horseback riding possibilities. Open year-round, 9.30-4; park fee: $3.00. For more information write *Malakoff Diggins State Historic Park*, North Bloomfield Star Rt., Box 852, Nevada City 95959; or call (916) 265-2740.

Plumas-Eureka State Park, County Road A-14, 4 miles west of Graeagle (off Hwy. 89 north). 6,749-acre park at 5,175-foot elevation, comprising pine forests, granite mountains, clear-water lakes and snowmelt creeks. It also contains an old mining town (Johnsville), a museum, several mine buildings and a five-story 60-stamp mill. In the park, too, is a pioneer ski area with one of the world's first ski lifts. The park offers good camping, picnicking, hiking and fishing; campground closed in winter. Park hours: 8-4 daily in summer; no day use fee. For more information call (916) 836-2380, or write *Plumas-Eureka State Park*, Johnsville Star Rt., Blairsden 96103.

THEATER. *Foothill Theatre Company;* housed in the old Nevada Theatre (1865) on Broad St., Nevada City. Features delicious comedy and drama, in spring, summer and fall. For reservations and program information, call (916) 265-TKTS, or write The Foothill Theatre Company, P.O. Box 1812, Nevada City 95959.

American Victorian Museum, 325 Spring St., Nevada City. Musical groups from around the world perform here — from pianists to violinists, and even flutists, folk singers and a variety of other musicians. Dining facilities on premises, and Victorian museum exhibits. For reservations call (916) 265-5804.

For classical music, try the *Music in the Mountains* group, which books some of the finest concerts and musicales. For program information and reservations call (916) 265-6124; or write Music in the Mountains, P.O. Box 1451, Nevada City 95959.

HISTORIC SACRAMENTO

"Gateway to the Gold Fields"

Sacramento is the state capitol of California. It is also a place rich in California history. It has at the center of it Old Sacramento—once the gateway to the gold fields—and a real frontier fort, several beautiful Victorian mansions, and a dozen or so superb museums devoted to the history, culture and arts of California. The city also has numerous other tourist attractions, and abundant good accommodations and restaurants, with fine shopping possibilities.

Sacramento lies approximately 70 miles northeast of San Francisco—or 20 miles or so west of the Gold Country towns of Auburn and Placerville—at the intersection of the all-important Interstates 80 and 5 and Highways 50 and 99. There is also a commercial airport here, just to the northwest of the city, and a smaller executive airport a little to the south of central Sacramento. Besides which, the city is linked by rail, both from the east and west.

DISCOVERING HISTORIC SACRAMENTO

We suggest you begin your tour of historic Sacramento where Sacramento itself began — at Sutter's Fort, corner of L and 26th streets. The fort dates from 1839, originally built by pioneer land baron, John Sutter, as the seat of his grand agricultural empire, New Helvetia, which comprised part of the Sierra Gold Country and upon which gold was first discovered in January of 1848. Sutter's Fort also has other historic associations: American pioneer John C. Fremont and his expedition party stayed here briefly in 1844; General Mariano Vallejo, the Mexican governor of California, was held captive here during the historic Bear Flag Revolt of 1846; and in 1847, survivors of the ill-fated Donner Party were brought here after being rescued from their winter campsites in the Sierras. Visitors can now tour the largely-restored fort, with its thick adobe walls enclosing a large compound with two or three buildings, including a worthwhile museum. Most of the rooms in the fort, too, have been restored to reflect their original function, such as a blacksmith shop, saddlery, bunkhouse, cooperage and distillery, among others; and during the "Living History" days, held each year in spring, you can experience the 1840s atmosphere, with the local rangers and docents sporting 19th-century costumes and recreating scenes from the mid-1800s.

Directly behind Sutter's Fort on K Street is the California State Indian Museum, with superb exhibits and artifacts from California's many diverse Indian cultures, all arranged by theme — such as nature, family, and spirituality — and with the past and present splendidly juxtaposed. Among the exhibits here you will find collections of basketry, old redwood canoes, bobcat pelts, pestles to grind acorns, and old photographs depicting ceremonial dances and contemporary tribal elders. The museum also presents a slide show on weekends.

West from Sutter's Fort and the State Indian Museum, on the landscaped Capitol Mall at the intersection of 10th Street (between L and N streets), stands the glorious, copper-domed State Capitol, one of the great tourist attractions of Sacramento, dating from 1874. It was recently, in 1982, restored at a cost of $68 million — believed to be one of the most extensive projects even undertaken in the U.S. to restore a single historic building. The Capitol building now stands at the center of a splendid, 40-acre park, with manicured lawns, trees and shrubs from around the world, including a collection from the Civil War battlefields — and monuments, fountains, flower bushes, and an experimental rose garden. The Capitol building itself is quite breathtaking, majestic white, with colonnades and classical statues, modeled after the nation's Capitol in Washington, D.C. Inside are crystal chandeliers, carved and polished mahogany furnishings, marble mosaic floors, gold leaf, fine leather, and antiques. There is a museum and other exhibit areas here, which can be toured, and when the Senate and Assembly are in session, you can see the State's legislators at work from their Legislative Chambers. Docent-guided tours are available during scheduled hours, between 9 a.m. and 5 p.m. daily, and in a theater in the basement a film on the restoration project is also shown.

Adjacent to the State Capitol on Capitol Mall is the California State Library, housed in an ornate, 1920s Greek-style granite building, and much to be recommended to visitors. The library boasts one of the largest collections of books in the state—including several old and rare books, gold-tooled and leather-bound, and numerous old manuscripts, letters, newspapers, histories, lithographs, photographs, and even portfolios of works by Ansel Adams, Edward Curtis and Eadweard Muybridge, among others—covering "all aspects of life in the state, from prehistoric times to present day." The library also has in it a Patent Library, Law Library, and a genealogical collection on California families; and in the general reading room here you can view a large wall mural by Maynard Dixon, completed in 1928, depicting the story and growth of California.

South of the Capitol on O Street, and also of interest, are the State Archives, with displays of such historic California documents as the original State Constitutions of 1848 and 1879; and a few blocks to the west of there, still on O Street, is another Sacramento gem, the Crocker Art Museum, believed to be the oldest art museum in the West. The Crocker Art Museum is housed in a splendid old mansion, dating from the 1870s, originally built by Sacramento Judge Edwin Bryant Crocker to house his prized art collection. The museum has in it—displayed on three floors of galleries—one of the finest collections of Western art by 19th-century painters, including paintings of scenes from the gold mines by Charles Nahl, and Sierra and Yosemite scenery and other landscapes by Albert Bierstadt. There is also a gift shop on the ground floor of the museum, and on Sunday afternoons you can enjoy chamber music concerts in the museum's well-appointed ballroom.

North of the State Capitol, too, on 16th and H streets is the grand old Governor's Mansion, housed in an impressive Victorian-Italianate with a cupola, dating from 1877. The mansion was home to 13 of California's governors, up to, and including, Ronald Reagan. The 15-room mansion is now a State Historical Landmark, open to public viewing. Guided tours are offered daily between 10 a.m. and 4 p.m.

Another historic relic worth visiting, two blocks west of the Capitol at the corner of 8th and N streets, is the virtually-unrestored, but nevertheless quite grand, two-story Stanford Mansion, built between 1857 and 1872, and once the home of California legend Leland Stanford—railroad magnate, State Governor, U.S. Senator, and founder of Stanford University. The mansion and its grounds are now part of the Stanford House State Historic Park, open to public tours on Tuesdays, Thursdays and Saturdays.

The great glory of Sacramento yet, is the historic and colorful Old Sacramento, situated on the banks of the Sacramento River, westward from the State Capitol, between Capitol Mall and I Street. Old Sacramento dates from the gold rush days, when it was important as the "gateway" to the Sierra gold country. It has in it no fewer than 60 splendid gold rush-era buildings, all restored to their former glory, and housing some 200 or so delightful shops, galleries and restaurants. Much of the rest of Old Sacramento, too, has been painstakingly restored, with wooden sidewalks, cobblestone streets, and antique gas lamps. There is even an 1870s railroad passenger terminal here, and

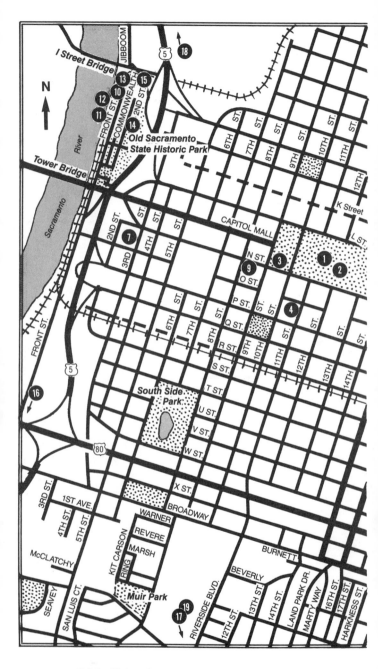

Points of Interest -

1) State Capitol
2) Capitol Park
3) State Library
4) State Archives
5) Sutters Fort

6) State Indian Museum
7) Crocker Art Museum
8) Governor's Mansion
9) Stanford House
10) State Railroad Museum

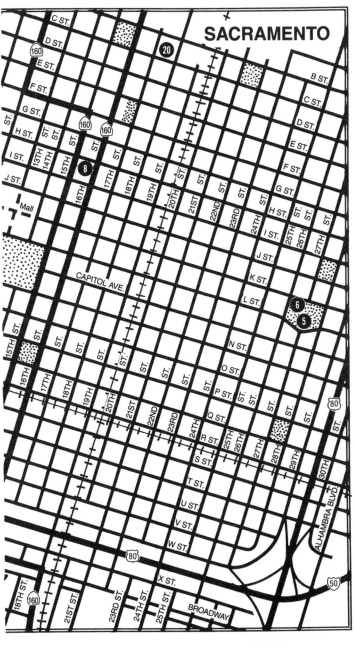

11) Central Pacific Passenger
    Station
12) Sacramento History Center
13) Big Four Building
14) Eagle Theatre
15) Huntington-Hopkins   Store

16) Towe Ford Museum
17) Sacramento Zoo
18) Discovery Park
19) Fairytale Town
20) Almond Growers Exchange

equally authentic, 19th-century steam trains, offering train rides on summer weekends, from Old Sacramento to the William Land Park, just to the south, and back, some 7 miles along the Sacramento River.

Of special interest in Old Sacramento, however, is the Sacramento History Center, a superb, 18,000-square-foot museum, filled with exhibits centered on the history of the Sacramento Valley, and itself located at the north end of the old town. There are five main galleries here, each focusing on a different part of the valley's history: the Topomorphology Gallery depicts the environmental history of the Sacramento Valley; the Community Gallery focuses on the history of the valley's pioneer settlers and Native Americans indigenous to the area; the Agricultural Technology Gallery traces the history of all the technological advancements in the area; the McClatchy Gallery features Eleanor McClatchy's collection of Gold Rush memorabilia and early newspapers; and the Human Dialogue Gallery has changing exhibits from the Center's various collections. There is also a small orientation theater here, which features a short film giving an overview of the Center's exhibits.

Another place of supreme tourist interest, directly north of the History Center, is the California State Railroad Museum, the largest of its kind in the country. It comprises a Central Pacific passenger station, dating from 1876, where you can relive the noise and clamor of a bygone railroad era, with the aid of an audio tour wand; and an expansive, 100,000-square-foot museum where 21 restored locomotives and rolling stock are on display—including a million-pound Southern Pacific locomotive—and hundreds of railroad artifacts.

Also in the Railroad Museum complex is the Big Four Building, where in 1861, the "Big Four"—Charles Crocker, Collis P. Huntington, Mark Hopkins and Leland Stanford—drew up the plans for the building of the transcontinental railroad. Another, the Huntington-Hopkins Hardware Store, is also located here. It was originally opened in 1855 by Collis Huntington and Mark Hopkins—two of the "Big Four"—to sell pick-axes, shovels, and hardware to miners during the gold rush; and it made them rich. Both the Hardware Store and the Big Four Building have been largely restored, and are open to public viewing.

Among other places to be recommended to visitors to Old Sacramento are the Eagle Theatre, dating from 1849, and where you can still enjoy plays and musicals from several different theater companies; and the B.F. Hastings Building, which in 1860 was the western terminus for the Pony Express, and which now has in it three small museums, each with its own historic significance. One of the museums recreates the first California Supreme Court in the 1850s, for it was here that the State Supreme Court convened from 1855 to 1857, and again from 1859 to 1869; another is a communications museum, with an early-day telegraph display, highlighting the building's function as an office for an 1800s telegraph company; and the third houses a Wells Fargo historical exhibit, also dating from the 1850s.

If time permits, try to also visit some of Sacramento's other attractions. The Sacramento Zoo, for one, is situated on the landscaped, 236-acre William Land Park on West Land Park Drive, near Sutterville Road, just to the south of the city center. It has in it a flamingo exhibit, a reptile house, and several species of wild animals, including lions and tigers. Also, across from the zoo is Fairytale Town, a small, 6-acre park, developed around Mother Goose rhymes and fairytales, and featuring ongoing puppet shows, especially interesting to children.

Other places of interest, north of downtown, include the well-liked Discovery Park, directly above the American River on Garden Highway, which has hiking, bicycling, picnicking, camping, fishing, swimming, a boat ramp, an archery range and an equestrian area; and the California Exposition on Exposition Boulevard, at the fairgrounds, where there is an aquatic park with several water-slides, racing and paddle boats, and a swimming pool.

For automobile enthusiasts, the best of all places to visit is the California Towe Ford Museum on Front Street, near Broadway. The museum houses some 150 Ford motor cars, representing every Ford model from 1903 to 1953. The museum is open daily, 10 a.m.-6 p.m.

Yet another place of tourist interest is the California Almond Growers' Exchange on C and 18th streets, notable as "the world's largest almond factory," comprising 20 buildings and 24 silos, and situated on a 90-acre site. Almonds, of course, are California's number one food product, with annual exports exceeding $1 billion; and the growers' exchange processes nearly 1.5 million of these nuts daily. Tours of the plant are offered on weekdays, at 9 and 10 a.m. and 1 and 2 p.m., highlighting the entire processing operation, from sorting the almonds to packing and sealing them in "airline packets." There is also a film—"The Amazing Almond"—shown at the plant theater; besides which, there is a gift shop on the premises, where you can buy almonds in every form and flavor.

To be also recommended to visitors to the area are two nearby attractions: the Old Town at Folsom, with its mid-19th-century atmosphere; and the University of California at Davis, situated on a 3,600-acre campus, believed to be the third largest campus in the state, and which features three art galleries, several museums, a large, state-of-the-art craft center, a world-famous arboretum, and a unique experimental farm. U.C. Davis lies 17 miles west on Interstate 80, and Folsom some 18 miles or so northeastward, also on Interstate 80.

PRACTICAL INFORMATION FOR HISTORIC SACRAMENTO

HOW TO GET THERE. By Air. The Sacramento Metropolitan Airport is located off I-5 north, at 6900 Airport Blvd., Sacramento airport phone: (916) 929-5411. The following airlines have regularly scheduled services to Sacramento: *American Airlines* (800) 433-7300/(916) 443-3399; *American West* (916) 448-8364; *United Airlines* (800) 631-1500/(916) 440-0270; *Continental* (800) 525-0280/(916) 369-2700; *Delta* (800) 221-1212/(916) 446-3464; *Northwest* (800) 225-2525; *U.S. Air* (800) 428-4322/(916) 922-8021.

By Train. *Amtrak* has daily passenger services to and from Sacramento, both eastward and westward. The train station is located at 4th and I Sts. For schedules and information, call (800) 872-7245/(916) 485-8506.

By Bus. *Greyhound Bus Lines.* Greyhound has daily scheduled services to Sacramento from most major cities; the Greyhound Bus Terminal is located at 715 L St., Sacramento. For schedules, fares and reservations, call (916) 444-6800.

By Road. Sacramento is situated at the junction of *Interstates 5* and *80* and *Highways 99* and *50*, approximately 85 miles from San Francisco, or 379 miles from Los Angeles. Several smaller routes also converge on Sacramento.

 ACCOMMODATIONS. Sacramento has abundant good accommodations, including five-star hotels, motels and bed and breakfast inns, many of them in the downtown area, quite close to Old Sacramento. Most of the area's hotels and motels accept credit cards; however, it is advisable to inquire with the respective establishment in advance. Rates, based on double occupancy, are categorized as follows: *Deluxe,* over $60; *Expensive,* $50-$60; *Moderate,* $35-$50; *Inexpensive,* under $35. (Note: rates are subject to change, and a sales tax will be added to your motel bill.)

The Sterling Hotel. *Deluxe.* 1300 H St., Sacramento; (916) 448-1300. Small elegant hotel, dating from 1894, located close to the State Capitol. 12 guest rooms, most with private jacuzzis. Glass conservatory behind the main house. Also restaurant on premises.

Beverly Garland Hotel. *Deluxe.* 1780 Tribute Rd., Sacramento; (916) 929-7900. 203 rooms, with TV and phones. Restaurant, coffee shop, and cocktail lounge.

Clarion Hotel. *Deluxe.* 700 16th St., Sacramento; (916) 444-8000. 239 rooms and suites, all with TV and phones. Restaurant, cocktail lounge, pool.

Courtyard by Marriott. *Deluxe.* 10683 White Rock Rd., Rancho Cordova; (916) 638-3800/(800) 321-2211. 145 rooms; TV, phones. Restaurant, cocktail lounge, and outdoor pool.

Hotel El Rancho. *Expensive-Deluxe.* 1029 W. Capitol, Sacramento; (916) 371-6731/(800) 952-5566 in CA. 250 rooms and suites; TV and phones. Restaurant, cocktail lounge, pool, spa and sauna. Also tennis and racquetball courts, and weight room.

Delta King. *Expensive.* At the Old Sacramento Wharf, 1000 Front St., Sacramento; (916) 444-5464. 44 staterooms on board an authentic sternwheeler. Restaurants and cocktail lounges on board; also shops.

Hilton Inn. *Deluxe.* 2200 Harvard, Sacramento; (916) 922-4700. 329 rooms with TV and phones. Two restaurants, 4 cocktail lounges. Heated outdoor pool.

Hyatt Regency Hotel. *Deluxe.* Cnr. 12th and L Sts., Sacramento; (800) 228-9000. 502 rooms and suites, with TV and phones. Restaurant and cocktail lounge; pool. Located across from the State Capitol.

Best Western Harbor Inn. *Expensive.* 1250 Halyard Dr., West Sacramento; (916) 371-2100/(800) 528-1234. 99 rooms, with TV, phones and wet bars. Restaurant, coffee shop, cocktail lounge.

Best Western Ponderosa Motor Inn. *Deluxe.* 1100 H St., Sacramento; (916) 441-1314/(800) 528-1234. 98 rooms with TV and phones. Restaurant, cocktail lounge, heated pool and sauna. Continental breakfast.

Best Western Heritage Inn. *Deluxe.* 11269 Point East Dr., Rancho Cordova; (916) 635-4040/(800) 641-1076. 127 rooms; TV, phones, some whirlpool tubs and wetbars with refrigerators. Restaurant and cocktail lounge on premises. Pool, spa, sauna, exercise room. Non-smoking rooms available.

Holiday Inn. *Deluxe.* 300 J St., Sacramento; (916) 446-0100. 368 rooms; TV and phones. Restaurant, pool.

Aunt Abigail's. *Deluxe.* 2120 G St., Sacramento; (916) 441-5007. 5 rooms with private baths, one with jacuzzi. Full, gourmet breakfast; evening wine.

Amber House. *Deluxe.* 1315 22nd St., Sacramento; (916) 444-8085. 6 guest rooms, 4 with private baths; phones, air conditioning. Antiques and stained glass; hot tub in the garden. Generous breakfast.

Driver Mansion Inn. *Deluxe.* 2019 21st St., Sacramento; (916) 455-5243. 8 rooms, most with jacuzzis and fireplaces. Full breakfast.

Hartley House. *Deluxe.* 700 22nd St., Sacramento; (916) 447-7829. Turn-of-the-century home with 5 rooms with private baths, including some clawfoot tubs; also phones. Full breakfast.

Briggs House. *Expensive-Deluxe.* 2209 Capitol Ave., Sacramento; (916) 441-3214. Restored Victorian home, dating from 1901. 7 rooms, 5 with private baths. Spa. Bicycles available for guest use. Gourmet breakfast.

TOURIST INFORMATION. Sacramento Chamber of Commerce, 917 7th St., Sacramento; (916) 443-3371. Brochures and information on area lodgings and restaurants, tours, seasonal events, and points of interest. Also maps.

Old Sacramento Visitors Center, 1104 Front St., Old Sacramento; (916) 442-7644. Old Sacramento tourist literature, including information on places of interest, walking tours and events in the old town.

California Office of Tourism, 1121 L Street, Suite 103, Sacramento; (916) 322-1396. Several tourist publications available, including The California Regions, California Visitors Map and The Californias Calendar of Events.

LOCAL TRANSPORTATION. Sacramento's *Regional Transit System* offers regular bus as well as light rail services throughout much of the city. For schedules and fare information, call (916) 321-BUSS.

Car Rentals. All major car rental companies have agencies in Sacramento. *Budget Rent-A-Car* (800) 527-0700/(916) 973-8411; *Thrifty Rent-A-Car* (800) 367-2277/(916) 447-2847; *Dollar* (800) 421-6868;(916) 489-3600; *Avis* (800) 331-1212/(916) 444-2311; *Hertz* (800) 654-3131/(916) 444-2414; *American International* (800) 527-0202/(916) 921-0555; *National Car Rental* (800) 328-4567/(916) 929-0205.

RV Rentals. *Cruise America,* 3479 Fitzgerald Rd., Rancho Cordova, (916) 635-7967; *Revco RV Center,* 3329 Fitzgerald Rd., Rancho Cordova, (916) 638-7024; *Travel Time RV Center,* 5910 Auburn Blvd., Citrus Heights, (916) 344-1383; *Rec Vee World/U-Haul,* 1650 El Camino Ave., Sacramento, (916) 929-2200; *Vacations R-Us,* (916) 962-0922.

SEASONAL EVENTS. February. *Mardi Gras.* Traditional Mardi Gras celebration, featuring music dancing, food, a parade, and food stalls. For schedule of events and more information, call (916) 443-7815.

March. *Camellia Festival.* Held during the first two weeks of the month. Celebration of Sacramento's official flower, with flower exhibits featuring over 10,000 blossoms, and a parade, regattas and other sporting events, and a grand ball. The festival dates from the 1950s. Festival information on (916) 442-7673.

April. *Living History Day at the State Capitol.* Docents and actors play characters from California's history. (916) 324-0333.

May. *Dixieland Jazz Jubilee.* Memorial weekend. Jazz performances in Old Sacramento and several other locations throughout the city; features over 100 bands from all over the world. (916) 372-5277.

July. *Old Sacramento 4th of July Celebration.* Living history days enactments, and a parade. (916) 443-7815. *Sacramento Water Festival.* 4th of July weekend. Powerboat and canoe races, nighttime Parade of Lights on the Sacramento River, spectacular fireworks display. (916) 442-8370.

August. *California State Fair.* Last two weeks of the month. At Cal Expo. 135-year-old state fair. Agricultural displays, horse racing, wine tasting, carnival, food concessions, and entertainment. (916) 924-2000. *Tomato Festival.* Held at Old Sacramento. Features games and entertainment, and food stalls. For more information, call (916) 443-7815.

September. *U.S. National Handcar Races.* Third weekend. Teams from all over the western U.S. compete in handcar races along a 300-meter length of railroad track in Old Sacramento. The racing handcars were designed and built at the California State Railroad Museum restoration shop. For a schedule and information, call (916) 445-7373.

October. *Living History Days.* Sutters Fort. Re-enactment of historical events by docents and rangers dressed in 19th-century costumes, (916) 445-4422. *Old Sacramento Historic Area Elections.* Old Sacramento. Merchants dress in period costumes and campaign for such offices as Mayor, Sheriff, Madam and Jailkeeper. (916) 443-7815. *Oktoberfest.* City-wide celebration, featuring German beer, food, music and dancing. (916) 481-4071.

November. *Indian Arts & Crafts Fair.* Held at the State Indian Museum. Features Native Indian handicrafts. For a schedule and more information, call (916) 324-0971.

December. *Victorian Christmas at the Old Governor's Mansion.* First weekend of the month. Tour of the Governor's Mansion, decorated for Christmas; choir singing, and Santa Claus.

 PLACES OF INTEREST. California State Capitol and Museum. 10th St. between L and N Sts. (Room B-27); (916) 324-0333. Free admission. Magnificent, copper-domed Capitol building, featuring colonnades and classical statues, modeled after the nation's Capitol. Museum and other exhibit areas open to the public. Also, 40-acre landscaped park, with manicured lawns, and trees and shrubs from around the world, including a collection from the Civil War battlefields. The State Capitol dates from 1874, and was restored in 1982 at a cost of $68 million. Guided tours daily, 9-5.

California State Railroad Museum. 111 I St. (cnr. 2nd St.); (916) 445-7373. Largest railroad museum in the country, comprising 100,000 square feet of museum space, and a restored 1876 Central Pacific Passenger Station. 21 restored locomotives and rolling stock on display, including a million-pound Southern Pacific locomotive, and hundreds of railroad artifacts. Open 10-5 daily; admission $3.00 adults, $1.00 children.

Towe Ford Museum of California. 2200 Front St.; (916) 442-6802. Automobile museum with some 150 Ford motor cars on display, representing every year of model from 1903 to 1953. Open daily, 10-6.

Crocker Art Museum. Cnr. O and 3rd Sts.; (916) 449-5423. Oldest art museum in the West, built in the 1870s to house Sacramento Judge Edwin Bryant Crocker's art collection. Features three floors of galleries, and one of the finest collections of Western art by 19th-century painters, among them Charles Nahl, Albert Bierstadt, Thomas Hill and William Keith. Also has a gift shop on the premises, and a well-appointed ballroom where chamber music concerts are presented on Sunday afternoons. Museum hours: 10-5 Wed.-Sun, 1-9 p.m. Tues. Admission: $2.00 adults, $1.00 children and seniors.

Eagle Theatre. 925 Front St.; (916) 446-6761. Pioneer theatre, dating from

1849. Features plays, musicals, and theater performances on weekends. Also, Parks Department-produced slide show daily, highlighting points of interest around the city. For show times and more information, call the theatre.

Stanford House. 800 N St.; (916) 324-0575. Partially restored, mid-1800s two-story mansion, formerly the home of Leland Stanford—railroad magnate, State Governor, U.S. Senator, and founder of Stanford University. The mansion is now part of the Stanford House State Historic Park. Public tours at 12.15 p.m. on Tuesdays and Thursdays, and 12.15 p.m. and 1.30 p.m. on Saturdays.

State Indian Museum. 2618 K St.; (916) 445-4209. Features exhibits and artifacts from California's many diverse Indian cultures. Displays include collections of basketry, old redwood canoes, bobcat pelts, pestles to grind acorns, and old photographs depicting ceremonial dances and tribal elders. Slide show on weekends. Open 10-5 daily; admission $1.00 adults, 50¢ children.

Sutters Fort. 2701 L St.; (916) 445-4209. Restored frontier fort, built in 1839 by pioneer land baron, John Sutter. Features a large compound enclosed by thick adobe walls, and a series of adobe buildings with rooms recreating their original function, such as a blacksmith shop, saddlery, cooperage, distillery, and prison, among others. Museum and interpretive center on premises. Open daily 10-5; admission $1.00 adults, 50¢ children.

Governor's Mansion. Cnr. 16th and H Sts. Charming, 15-room Victorian mansion, dating from 1877. The mansion has been home to 13 California governors, including Ronald Reagan. Open daily 10-5; guided tours 10-4. Admission: $1.00 adults, 50¢ children.

Sacramento History Center. 101 I St. (cnr. Front St.); (916) 449-2057. Superb, 18,000-square-foot museum, filled with exhibits centered on the history of the Sacramento Valley. Houses five main galleries, each focusing on a different aspect of the valley's history—the environmental history, the history of the valley's pioneer settlers and Native Americans, the history of all technological advances in the area, and Gold Rush memorabilia. Open 10-5 daily; tours at 11 a.m. and 2 p.m. Admission fee: $3.00 adults, $1.00 children.

State Archives. 1020 O St.; (916) 455-4293. Displays of historic California documents, including the State Constitutions of 1848 and 1879. Open 8-5, Mon.-Fri.

State Library. 914 Capitol Mall; (916) 322-4570. The state's largest and best-stocked library, with one of the most extensive collections of books in California—"covering all aspects of life in the state, from prehistoric times to present day." The library also houses a Patent Library, Law Library, a genealogical collection on California's families, and a general reading room with a superb wall mural by Maynard Dixon, completed in 1928. Library hours: 8-5, Mon.-Fri.

Sacramento Zoo. 3930 West Land Park Dr.; (916) 449-5885. Situated on the 236-acre, landscaped William Land Park. Features a flamingo exhibit, reptile house, and several species of wild animals, including lions and tigers. Open 9-4 Mon.-Fri., 9-5 Sat.-Sun. Admission: $3.00 adults, $1.50 children on weekdays, and $3.50 adults, $2.00 children on weekends.

Fairytale Town. Cnr. Land Park Dr. and Sutterville Rd.; (916) 449-5233. Small, 6-acre park, developed around Mother Goose nursery rhymes and fairytales, and featuring on-going puppet shows. Open daily. 10-4.30. Admission: $1.75 adults, $1.25 children on weekdays, and $2.00 adults, $1.50 children on weekends.

Waterworld USA. At the Fairgrounds, 1600 Exposition Blvd.; (916) 924-0555. Features a variety of water slides, racing and paddle boats, and a swimming pool. Open daily May-Sept.; admission $10.95 adults, $8.95 children.

Blue Diamond Almond Exchange. Cnr. 17th and C Sts.; (916) 446-8409. Billed as "the world's alrgest almond factory," where approximately 1.5 million almonds are processed daily. Tours Mon.-Fri. at 9 and 10 a.m., 1 and 2 p.m. Free admission and tasting; gift shop on premises.

 **TOURS.** **Walking Tours.** Guided, history-oriented tours of Old Sacramento, conducted by State Park docents. Tours depart from the Central Pacific Passenger Station on Front St.; weekends only. For more information, call (916) 322-3676.

Horse Drawn Carriage Tours. Tours of Old Sacramento, aboard horse-drawn carriages. For fares and schedules, call (916) 443-7962.

Rail Tours. Departing from Central Pacific Railroad Freight Depot on Front St. 7-mile round trips along the Sacramento River, on board authentic steam trains. Trains operate on the hour, 10-5, weekends and holidays (except 4th of July weekend) from May until Labor Day. Fare: $3.00 adults, $2.00 children; ages 5 and under free. For reservations and information, call (916) 448-4466.

 BOAT CRUISES. **River City Queen.** River Bank Marina, 1401 Garden Hwy.; (916) 921-1111. Cruises down the Sacramento River on a paddlewheeler. Boats operate Wed.-Sun. in summer, Fri.-Sun. rest of the year. Pleasure cruises $10.00 adults, $5.00 children; brunch cruises $15.50 adults, $10.50 children. Reservations required.

Matthew McKinley. L Street Landing, 1207 Front St.; (916) 441-6481. Sacramento River boat cruises. Sightseeing tours $10.00 adults, $5.00 children; dinner cruises $12.50-$17.50 (not including meal); also lunch and brunch cruises. Reservations recommended.

 RESTAURANTS. Dining out in Sacramento is generally good to excellent in the better restaurants, with a wide variety of cuisines, including Continental, California, Chinese, Japanese, Italian and Mexican; even pizza parlors and fast-food outlets are plentiful in the area.

Restaurant prices — on the basis of full-course dinner, excluding drinks, tax and tips — are categorized as follows: *Deluxe,* over $20; *Expensive,* $15-$20; *Moderate,* $10-$15; *Inexpensive,* under $10.

California Fats. *Expensive.* 1015 Front St.; (916) 441-7966. Specializing in California-Pacific cuisine. Open for lunch Mon.-Sat., dinner daily; also brunch on Sundays.

Fat City Bar & Cafe. *Moderate-Expensive.* 1001 Front St., (916) 446-6768. Large, continental-style cafe, with century-old mahogany bar. Open for lunch and dinner daily, brunch on weekends.

Pilot House Restaurant. *Expensive.* 1000 Front St.; (916) 444-9666. Restaurant located on board the Delta King paddlewheeler, in Old Sacramento. Serving Continental and California cuisine. Lunch and dinner daily. Reservations suggested.

Sakura Sushi Train. *Moderate.* 1111 2nd St.; (916) 448-8334. Teppan, tempura and yakitori, also excellent sushi bar. Lunch Tues.-Fri., dinner Tues.-Sun.

Annabelle's Family Restaurant. *Moderate.* 200 J St.; (916) 448-6239. Casual, family-style restaurant, serving primarily pasta and pizza. Open for lunch and dinner daily.

Fulton's Prime Rib. *Expensive.* 900 2nd St.; (916) 444-9641. Prime rib, and seafood and lamb specialties. Open for lunch and dinner daily.

Los Padres. *Inexpensive-Moderate.* Cnr. J St. and the Embarcadero; (916) 443-6376. Authentic Mexican cooking. Lunch and dinner daily.

Jon Pierpoint Daley. *Expensive.* 926 2nd St.; (916) 446-7736. Steaks, seafood and ribs. Cocktail lounge. Open for lunch and dinner daily. Reservations suggested.

The Firehouse. *Expensive.* 1112 2nd St.; (916) 442-4772. Restaurant housed in historic, Old Sacramento firehouse, dating from 1853. Featuring Continental specialties. Delightful, shaded brick-paved courtyard for outdoor dining. Open for lunch Mon.-Fri., dinner Mon.-Sat. Reservations recommended.

Cafe La Salle. *Expensive-Deluxe.* 1028 2nd St.; (916) 442-9000. Gourmet California-French cuisine; extensive wine list. Elegant setting. Open for lunch and dinner daily. Reservations advised.

The Bull Market. *Expensive-Deluxe.* 815 11th St.; (916) 446-6757. Well-appointed Sacramento restaurant, serving primarily Continental cuisine. Flambé specialties; live jazz, Thurs.-Sun. Open for dinner daily.

GOLD MINING TOOLS

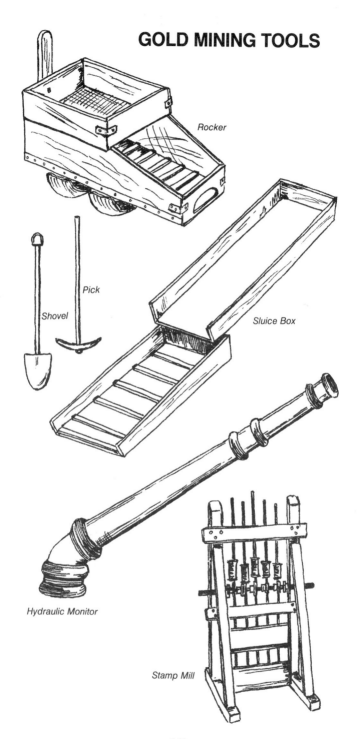

Rocker

Sluice Box

Shovel

Pick

Hydraulic Monitor

Stamp Mill

140

HOW TO PAN GOLD

(1)

(1)

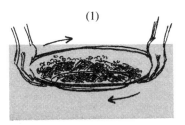

Use flat-bottomed pan with gently sloping sides. Fill pan with dirt and water and swirl around for several minutes. Gold gradually settles to the bottom.

(2)

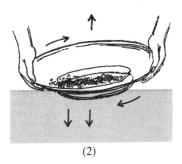

Now lift pan just above the water, tilting it and swirling at the same time. Lighter sand washes away over the sides, leaving only the heavier, gold residue at the bottom of the pan.

(2)

CALIFORNIA'S GOLD PRODUCTION
(1848-1874)

Year	Gold Produced	Year	Gold Produced
1848	$ 245,301	1862	$38,854,668
1849	$10,151,360	1863	$23,501,736
1850	$41,273,106	1864	$24,071,423
1851	$75,938,232	1865	$17,930,858
1852	$81,294,700	1866	$17,123,867
1853	$67,613,487	1867	$18,265,452
1854	$69,433,493	1868	$17,555,867
1855	$55,485,395	1869	$18,229,044
1856	$57,509,411	1870	$17,458,133
1857	$43,628,172	1871	$17,477,885
1858	$46,591,140	1872	$15,482,194
1859	$45,846,599	1873	$15,019,210
1860	$44,095,163	1874	$17,264,836
1861	$41,884,995		

INDEX

The abbreviation SGC stands for Southern Gold Country.
The abbreviation NGC stands for Northern Gold Country.
The abbreviation SAC stands for Sacramento.